For The
Unremembered

For The Unremembered

A Journey of Reflection into Cape Cod's Connection to Slavery

Susanna Graham-Pye

Foreword by Lynne A. Rhodes
PRESIDENT, NAACP CAPE COD

SCHIFFER PUBLISHING

4880 Lower Valley Road • Atglen, PA 19310

Other Schiffer Books on Related Subjects:

The Cape Cod National Seashore: A Photographic Adventure & Guide,
Christopher Seufert, 978-0-7643-3995-0
In My Footsteps: A Cape Cod Traveler's Guide, Second Edition,
Christopher Setterlund, 978-0-7643-6667-3
Lost History of the North Shore: Little Known Tales from Massachusetts,
Christopher Forest, 978-0-7643-3568-6

Library of Congress Control Number: 2024946205

Cover and book design by Danielle D. Farmer
Front cover and title page photograph by Ryan Johnson
Front cover map by Walter M. Gaffney

Courtesy www.bigstockphoto.com: The historic landmark pilgrim monument and town hall rising above provincetown massachusetts on a new england autumn day © tempestz. Cranberries floating in a bog on a farm in South Yarmouth, Massachusetts on a sunny blue sky day in Cape Cod © tempestz. The Highland Lighthouse against a beautiful dramatic sunset in North Truro Massachusetts on the Cape Cod National Seashore © tempestz. SANDWICH, MASSACHUSETTS - JULY 14, 2016: Tourists walk across the Sandwich Boardwalk at Mill Creek MA. Sandwich first settled in 1637 is the oldest town on Cape Cod © Radomir Rezny
Courtesy of www.vectorstock.com: Silhouettes of lighthouse vector image © octopusgraphic. Set of vintage ships vector image ©Kasyanov. Temple vector image © fet. Decoration elegance horned object shadow buck vector image © Kolesnikov90. Silhouette lighthouse on a light background vector image © Serz72. Black and white ink sketch of vintage vector image c webadgood, Small plane monochrome isolated vector image c desaintcorp, Hand drawn forest fir trees silhouettes vector image © Nadzin.

Type set in American Scribe/Abril Text

ISBN: 978-0-7643-6909-4
ePub: 978-1-5073-0529-4
Printed in India

Published by Schiffer Publishing, Ltd.
4880 Lower Valley Road
Atglen, PA 19310
Phone: (610) 593-1777; Fax: (610) 593-2002
Email: info@schifferbooks.com
Web: www.schifferbooks.com

MIX
Paper | Supporting responsible forestry
FSC www.fsc.org FSC™ C016779

For our complete selection of fine books on this and related subjects, please visit our website at www.schifferbooks.com. You may also write for a free catalog.

Schiffer Publishing's titles are available at special discounts for bulk purchases for sales promotions or premiums. Special editions, including personalized covers, corporate imprints, and excerpts, can be created in large quantities for special needs. For more information, contact the publisher.

For the other six goat
walkers, Tom, Mum,
and D.O.D.

Contents

Foreword

Folklore, which comes from historical facts and is passed down through storytelling, has often been ignored by historians who did not want to leave a reminder of the less-than-pleasant facts of Cape Cod's history. As a segment of society has attempted to eliminate history to reflect an artificial representation of culture, brave women and men have taken up the torch to write more inclusive and often less savory accounts of our past.

Organizations and reporting efforts, such as the Zion Union Heritage Museum Inc., the Atlantic Black Box Project, the Mashpee Nine, and Journeys into the Light movies, among others, are dedicated to researching and recording the significant and important history that is often omitted. This history is in danger of being lost as the traditionalist and baby boomer generations pass away. Even before the COVID-19 pandemic, communities had begun drifting away from gathering to listen to the Matriarchs and Patriarchs share the stories of generations that came before them.

Susanna Graham-Pye is a woman who recognized the importance of having a historical, written document. This book is a small piece of that history. She has taken the time and care to preserve some of this folklore, hidden in documents, resources, and public records. This book is dense with information and requires multiple reads to fully absorb. I found myself stopping to reflect on the stories I heard as a child—stories my classmates did not hear because their knowledge was shaped by an agenda meant to hide the less savory parts of Cape Cod history.

Classmates who did not look like me might not comprehend, even today, the truth that "roses have thorns." This is not to cast a shadow on Cape Cod history, but to include a piece of history that also needs to be understood. Please read and remember that roses need to be handled with care.

The Zion Union Heritage Museum Inc. was formed in response to the comment "Do Black people live on Cape Cod?" Yes, we do. And we share some of the same dark history of the Wampanoag and Aquinnah tribes of being traded as slaves. The Cape Cod Chapter of NAACP (National Association for the Advancement of Colored People) was created in 1961. I have served as president since 2022. When I was asked to read this, I was also asked to point out anything that seemed insensitive to marginalized communities. My eye did not spot anything, but if something was missed, I hope the oversight is forgiven. This is an enormous mission, and volumes are waiting to be written. Prepare for a journey into the past.

—LYNNE A. RHODES
President, NAACP Cape Cod

Introduction

THE IDEA

The root of this book lies in three different places. The first is with my mother. She worked as a middle school special education teacher. In Massachusetts, in middle school, students used to cover the American Revolution through the beginning of the Civil War. My mother always said it bothered her that people of African descent, those who were enslaved, were completely absent from the schoolbook pages of history, unless it was within the context of their enslavement, the abolition movement, and the Civil War. "African Americans worked to build this nation as much as any other person," she'd say. It bothered her immensely that Emancipation Day was not a national holiday. She wrote a letter to President Barack Obama, suggesting that January 1 be a national holiday as much for its new year beginnings as for the new beginnings for the nation. I don't know if she ever sent her letter, though I imagine she did. I do know she would be pleased that the nation now observes Juneteenth.

The second thing that grew the idea was the work I did for many years as a journalist. I worked for a number of small, independently owned local newspapers. I was blessed to work during a time when these small papers were not owned by one enormous media outlet, when the role of journalism in democracy—the need for a free, independent, unbiased press—existed as it should. That's a different conversation for another day. The point is that my favorite aspect of that job was writing features about the people, alive and dead, who made our community what it is. Everyone has a story, an interesting one. And in my years of writing, I often investigated the history of Cape Cod, setting scenes and giving depth to the stories of the Cape Codders I was interviewing. When it comes to the people of European Caucasian descent on the Cape, finding almost anything out about their pasts is possible. And yet, there were many people simply left out of the pages of history. That bothered me, probably because my mother had planted the seed of thought about others left out—intentionally or, even worse, unintentionally because they weren't considered a part of the story.

Coming full circle, I, like my mother, wound up working at a middle school. When my daughters were babies, I stayed home, freelancing. When they got to school age, the face of local media had changed in the brief few years I'd been away. They were laying off employees or not hiring, and I needed to find another job. One company had purchased many of the papers for which I'd worked. And so, I went to work at a local public charter school founded by the teachers with whom my mother had worked. What I envisioned as the last of three strands braided into the thinking that became this book was a conversation I had with a friend and colleague, Gary Clarke. We were standing on the playground during recess, and he said, "I've been trying to figure out how to prioritize the places I want to go." We chatted about getting older, time passing more and more quickly—there were so many places to see, so little time.

"I decided I'm going to identify some of my heroes and try to go to stand in the places they once stood," Gary told me. He gave Independence Hall in Philadelphia as an example of a place where he'd been and marveled at those who'd stood in the same place. I thought of standing in front of the Lincoln Memorial and imagining the Rev. Dr. Martin Luther King Jr. standing there too. And then I thought of all those people we'd never know were here, where we live—of the many people enslaved right here on Cape Cod. Their stories, their presence in building this country, deserve to be told. When we stand somewhere, those individuals deserve at the very least our knowledge they once stood here too.

LANGUAGE

As a teacher and a journalist I have always tried to put people, rather than labels, first. When speaking of people of different races, I have always tried to say "people who are [fill in the blank]": of African descent, of Chinese descent; people who were Indigenous to an area; people who learn differently; people who move with physical challenges. You name it, I try to put the word "people" or "person" first, underscoring that we are all people of different ancestry. Race is a cultural construct; one many argue was developed for the sole purpose of devaluing one population over another. In the case of writing this book, I speak often of people who were enslaved—and the people who enslaved them. At times it feels awkward, but it serves a purpose, reminding us that those who were enslaved were people, but so too were the people who enslaved them. There were the people from Europe who came to this region as colonists, and there were the people who had always lived here, the people whose ancestors had lived on Cape Cod for thousands of years. Again, this phrasing is lengthy and uses more words than a convenient identifying label, but it's important, I believe, both in terms of conveying the reality and because each time I build a sentence about who someone was or is, I have to stop and think about what I'm saying, remembering what is unremembered when I use easy labels applied with little thought. So, I apologize if there are moments of awkwardness in my sentence structure, but I hope that awkwardness makes you, the reader, stop and think too.

CAVEAT

While I did a large amount of research for my writing, I approached it as I would any story, seeking out information from the experts. I am not a researcher by vocation, nor do I think of myself as an expert. Thankfully, many incredible scholars and researchers are carefully combing through the past, teasing out what little information exists about those who were unremembered and helping to add more accurate pages to history books. This is also not to say that scholarship has not existed about slavery in early colonial days in the North for a very long time. Historians, researchers, and archivists have for years had a full picture of New England's involvement in the history of human trafficking. It's the general public, in classrooms and coffee shops, at family celebrations, where people are shocked to learn there were those among our storied forefathers who enslaved people. Here, my purpose is to offer a broad overview of Cape Cod's connection to and role in building human trafficking into the robust, brutal industry it was and still is.

Each chapter explores a different aspect of New England's part in bringing people here with the intention of, one way or another, profiting from their enslavement, and how Cape Codders were connected to that enterprise. I hope readers make a pilgrimage, using this book as a guide only—that people read a chapter and travel to a town, go to a spot, look out over the landscape, and ask some of the questions I have asked myself and have asked here on these pages. For each chapter, I have tried to include the name of at least one person who was enslaved in the area about which I'm writing. Names, like all words, are important. Throughout my research I have stumbled upon nameless people, identified only as "negro boy," "negro girl," "negro servant," "my negroes," and similar terms. When census taking became more firmly practiced, people in many cases were not given names but numbers. Rarely can we find a grave marker with the name of someone who was enslaved; they are missing. Most of all, I hope more and more people will start to search for answers to help fill in the blanks and tell the stories of those who were unremembered and deserve remembrance.

Map of Cape Cod

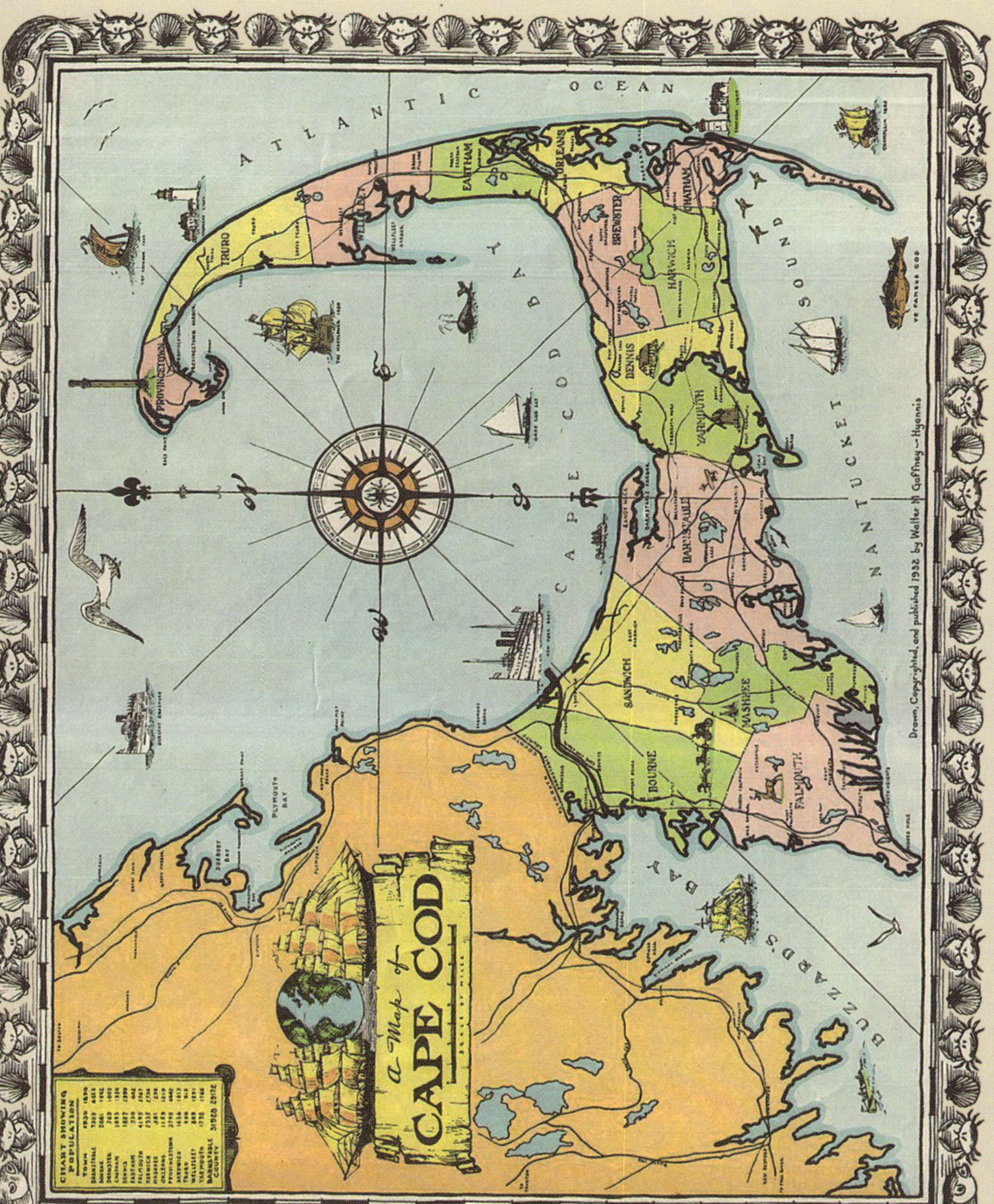

Map by Walter M. Gaffney

Prologue

Large peat beds occasionally reveal themselves on both the bay and ocean sides of the Cape. The peat often holds impressions from the past: footprints, horseshoe prints, and tracks from the wagons used to haul salt hay for the winter. *Photo by Susanna Graham-Pye*

Resonance from past events lies in the landscapes we inhabit. We can feel that echo, hear it, if we try. At least I believe we can. I love the word "resonance." It's one that sounds like what it means. Most folks associate resonance with the timbre of sound—for example, the depth and emotional texture of your grandmother's voice, the longing in the cry of a mourning dove cooing to her mate, or the heaving breath of the ocean. In all the talk, rustles, thunders, whispers, and sighs around us, there is a depth of sound. That is the resonance of the past in the landscape.

Landscapes speak to us if we're willing to listen. Listening and hearing are different. First, we hear. We are always hearing something: our own thoughts that might pull us from the voices of those around us; the stories of those around us that, for a moment, might drown out our thoughts. There is hearing, but then there is listening. Listening has intention. And if we stop to listen, the landscape has stories to tell. There are the winding bits of stone wall, wending their way through space where the need for walls has long since passed. Broken remnants of buildings—graffiti covered, startling—might loom in places where there is otherwise nothing. The ocean, with her never-ending push and pull, both buries and reveals our stories. After scraping away the sands, beds of peat crisscrossed with wagon tracks are revealed. A midden is uncovered on a construction site. We can

recognize the kinds of trees surrounding us, what they replaced, and why the others disappeared. The fertility of the soil on which we stand, or its barrenness, has a story too, as do the rivers that run through it all, or not, and the proximity to oceans, or not. Everything around us tells us how we got here.

And so, we can stand in places and hear the traffic passing, the plane overhead, the wind in the trees, and the voices of nearby neighbors and let it go at that. Or, we can truly and openly be in places, notice and listen to stories each tells, and feel the resonance of the past.

In these pages, the resonance to which I refer is the noticing of what is resonant, then the reflection about the prolongation of a lingering vibration left by the past. This book is about going to places armed with knowledge, standing in each, and coming full circle to be aware of the sounds, and smells, the sky, and the distant sound of the ocean—but to do so standing in someone else's shoes. At the end of each chapter, a number of locations are given. Each has a brief overview, and each is just one of many spots where people can contemplate and honor the existence of those who were unremembered.

CHAPTER 1

Sandwich—Beginnings

Âs Nutayuneân. We still live here . . . we are Wôpanâak, which means easterners. We are the people of the first light.

—Camille Madison,

a Wôpanâak Language Reclamation Project instructor

The Sandwich Boardwalk overlooks the marsh that drew the earliest European settlers to the area. For thousands of years prior to their arrival, the marsh offered food to the people who were native to the area. *Photo courtesy of* Cape Cod Life

In early August, with air softened by humid southwesterly winds, the salt marshes of Sandwich, Cape Cod, sprawl, lush and green, beneath periwinkle blue skies. August passes, and more frequent, northerly breezes turn colors crisp and bright. Fall finds the fields of salty marsh grasses rising from their boggy peat, clinging to summer's verdancy—but only for a moment. Ultimately, the marsh gives way as it always has, shifting to a golden shimmer under the lowering light of shortened days. Like the horizon at sunset, the progression of color deepens, darkens, and dulls—until, finally, winter descends. Under heavy gray skies, the marsh continues its daily dance with the tides, wearing its dry winter coat.

History and decay layer to build the foundation of the marsh. Day in, day out, season by season, year after year, the marsh has collected the detritus of decades. It is the birthplace of ocean fish, shellfish, and plankton—a nursery for the oceans of the world. It is the resting place of those that live there, the vegetation that dies there. The marsh is a place of birth and death, and those willing to listen will hear its stories on the whisper of the rippling grasses, in the trickle of water, in the clicking and bubbling of crabs, and in the wild calls of birds—egrets and waterfowl, oystercatchers and osprey. Traces of past people and place—the impressions of shod horses and the wheels of the wagons they hauled, where the shore once lay versus where it is today, records of changing sea levels—for the most part lie hidden beneath migrating sands. But bits and pieces are revealed by storm winds and tides. Their presence reminds us that what is today the beach and shorefront was once a marsh. The Great Marsh surrounding Sandwich is older than the Cape's other marshes and has been building upward for at least 3,700 years.

For the Wampanoag people, who have lived along the Cape's shifting coastline for more than ten thousand years, the marsh is and was a part of a larger picture. Long, long before European settlers arrived, the people who first populated this area moved with the seasons, using different parts of the landscape at different times for different reasons. In the fall, the Wampanoag people who inhabited what Europeans called Cape Cod went to the edges of the embayments behind barrier beaches, where marshes are fed with inwardly flowing channels. Many of these tidal waters turn brackish and ultimately lead to freshwater ponds that are the spawning grounds for anadromous fish. There, in the channels, the people would bury their "canoes" deep in the mud. While there, they harvested marsh grasses and reeds to weave thick mats for winter homes. As the weather turned and winter arrived, the Wampanoag people moved away from the shore to strong, sturdy homes built in deep kettle holes carved by the last glaciers that shaped this area. They tucked their homes into those deep hollows, which offered additional shelter as the prevailing northerly winds roared overhead, not bothering to waste time following the contour of the land too closely. In the spring, people moved closer to the shores, some people digging up the canoes while others harvested the running fish: shad, salmon, and herring.

There has always been food to be found in the marsh: clams, mussels, and oysters; tidal channels and sheltered waterways offer up striped bass and bluefish. Fresh water could be found there in the seeps as the peninsula's ground waters journeyed to the sea.

It is precisely the natural resources, especially the vast marsh, that drew Edmund Freeman to leave what is today Saugus in Massachusetts Bay Colony with ten other families to settle Sandwich in Plymouth Bay Colony. As it always shared its abundance in so many ways, the marsh offered ready-made food for sheep and cows. The animals could graze freely during the warmer months, and the salt hay could be harvested and dried on staddles for the winter months. The grasses were also used for thatched roofs, and taller reeds were used for caning furniture. Freeman and the others arrived in 1637; two years later, sixty families were living in Sandwich. The town had its own gristmill, was building a townhouse for civic affairs, and was thriving.

Sandwich is a town of firsts; it was the so-called first town established on Cape Cod and one of the first and now oldest Quaker communities. The first post built by the Pilgrims for trading with the people native to the area and Dutch explorers was on land that now lies in Bourne but was Sandwich then. It was a place called home by people of the first light, because they were the first to see the sun rise. Sandwich was located in Massachusetts, also home to Boston, from which the first colonial slave ships departed and where the first colonial rules were enacted that made enslavement of people legal.

Sandwich was the first town on Cape Cod to officially record the enslavement of people by one of its residents. In 1678, Canootus, Syman, and Joell—three men who were natives of the area—were arrested for breaking into the home of Zachariah Allen. The young men pried open a chest in Allen's home and stole £25. By the time the trio was arrested, the money was long gone. Because the men were not able to repay Allen, Josiah Winslow, the governor of New Plymouth presiding over the colonial court proceedings held in Marshfield, sentenced the three men to perpetual slavery. John Alden witnessed and signed the document.[1] The sentence suggests that Allen sell the men as a means of recovering the money stolen from him. If Allen could not sell them, and if they were ever found breaking the law again, Canootus and Symon were to be sold "out of the country." (Why not Joell?)

Enslavement among Indigenous peoples in New England was not unheard of. People taken captive during conflicts might be used for labor, but those occurrences were not permanent, nor was enslavement a condition they passed down through generations. On the other hand, Europeans' enslavement of the peoples who lived in New England started almost immediately upon the two groups' first encounters. Enslavement of Native people was quickly threaded into the fabric of early colonial life and economics. After the Pequot War, sparked by the struggle to control the trade of fur and wampum, the enslavement of the Indigenous people of New England slowed for a short time, but it resumed in earnest leading up to, during, and after King Philip's War. The war, bloody and violent, had only just ended when Canootus, Syman, and Joell broke into Allen's house. By the time the three men were sentenced, the practice of enslavement in Massachusetts had been codified for nearly thirty years. The enslavement by European colonists of people quickly turned into a permanent reality, passed down through generations like a genetic illness.

Legal enslavement in Massachusetts Bay Colony was formalized in 1641 with the Massachusetts Body of Liberties, written by John Winthrop, governor of the colony at the time and an enslaver himself. The law stated:

> There shall never be any bond slavery villainage or captivity amongst us unless it be lawful captives taken in just wars, and such strangers as willingly

sell themselves or are sold to us. And these shall have all the liberties and Christian usages which the law of God established in Israel concerning persons doth morally require. This exempt non from servitude who shall be judged thereto by Authority.[2]

Very little time passed before the practice of enslavement evolved into the true commercial enterprise it was in other established colonies. Winthrop's brother-in-law, Emanuel Downing, wrote a letter to the governor summarizing the prevailing attitudes of those who were in the business of colonizing, an enterprise ultimately and undeniably an economic endeavor:

> If upon a just war the Lord should deliver [the Pequots] into our hands, we might easily have men, women and children enough to exchange for Moores [black Africans], which will be more gainful pillage for us than we conceive, for I do not see how we can thrive until we get into a stock of slaves sufficient to do all our business, for our children's children will hardly see this great Continent filled with people, so that our servants will still desire freedom to plant for themselves and not to stay but for very great wages. And I suppose you know very well how we shall maintain 20 Moores cheaper than one English servant. The ships that shall bring Moores may come home laden with salt which may bear most of the charge, if not all of it."[3]

The first recorded people in Massachusetts who were Africans captured for trafficking arrived aboard the ship *Desire* in Boston Harbor in 1638.

Sandwich is a town of firsts, and beginnings are challenging and complex. Beginnings are often endings as well, and while the colonialists

The engraving shown here is of Alice, whose parents were from Barbados. Alice was born in Philadelphia and died in Bristol, Pennsylvania. Like Jean, Alice was enslaved and forced to begin her life anew on the basis of the decisions made by her enslavers. If records are correct, Alice lived to be older than 100 years old. Even if Jean and others enslaved on colonial Cape Cod had lived to be 100, most would not have had the chance to live in a nation, or world, without government-protected enslavement.

meticulously recorded their firsts—the first churches, first legal codes, first settlers of each colony—much of what ended was not so carefully preserved. In those fragile spaces that hang between beginnings and endings, much gets lost. One example of this—and of the lives of many who were enslaved and unremembered in New England—is Jean.

On an August day in 1738 in Sandwich, roughly one hundred years after the first enslaved people from Africa arrived in Massachusetts, Jean's life as she knew it ended, and a new series of firsts started as she began a new life in a new town, enslaved to a different family in a different home. Jean was born somewhere around 1716, if we can believe the bill of sale between Jonathan Bourne of Sandwich and Thomas Spooner of Plymouth, in which Bourne describes Jean as his "mulatto girl . . . being about 22 years of age." Bourne further asserts that he doesn't "know of any bodily sickness weakness or lameness that attends the . . . girl excepting her being with child."[4]

While so many details about Jean's life are unknown, we do know it was shaped by the rise and fall of the tides and changing seasons. In New England, unlike the South, most who were enslaved lived and worked side by side with their enslavers. Because the majority of those living in New England were Puritan, the vast majority of people living in enslavement were expected to live and worship as their enslavers did. Through records we know, too, that more women were enslaved in New England, as well as older men. Stronger, younger, healthy men wound up on sugar plantations down south.

The weather and seasons dictated the daily lives of the people on Cape Cod, and the weather and season crafted the tasks filling Jean's days. Preparing for winter was, of course, autumn's chore. Making the winter's supply of candles was "a household duty and a hard one too, for the great kettles

The silk of the milkweed pod was once wound into wicks by colonial women making candles. Candle making was an important fall task, with the dwindling light brought by the changing seasons. On the Cape, women harvested wax from a variety of sources, including honeycombs and bayberries. A bayberry candle, said to give off a lovely fragrance and made from local berries and wicks of milkweed silk, gives a deeper meaning to the term "locally sourced."
Photo by Susanna Graham-Pye

were tiresome and heavy to handle." Wicks could be woven from hemp, cotton, or the silk of milkweed pods.[5]

Huge pots were hung on trammels, iron hooks hanging from a lug pole, to be filled with water and tallow. Candles were dipped around wicks or hand-shaped and stored in candle boxes. Jean might have made candles from bayberries. Large numbers of the tiny berries were gathered and then thrown into boiling water, which removed their waxy exterior. This was skimmed and remelted. "This tallow is dearer than common tallow, but cheaper than wax. Candles of this do not easily bend nor melt in summer as common candles do; they burn better and slower, nor do they cause any smoke and yield a rather agreeable smell when they are extinguished."[6] Bees were kept as much for their wax as their honey.

The seasons that still drive daily life on Cape Cod—today built largely upon tourism and fishing—were paramount in dictating daily chores during colonial times. There were grains to be harvested, dried, and ground. Fish was dried, salt hay cut and dried. Before mills were built, grains were ground by hand. Windmills followed, making the task easier. Settlers grew corn, beans, flax, rye, and vegetables. They planted vineyards and gathered the wild strawberries, blackberries, blueberries, and grapes that grew throughout the region. Jean would have helped with spinning and weaving—flax for linens, and wool, which needed carding—for clothes. Fulling was done at home until communities built fulling mills. In short, before she left Sandwich for Plymouth, Jean certainly worked alongside all the others of the area to build the strong communities that grew into the colony of Massachusetts.

We know that in New England, while Jean's enslavement was legal, so too was her protection under the law. In an odd juxtaposition that led to the end of slavery in the state far earlier than in other parts of the country, all the legal protections offered to colonists extended to those who were enslaved as well. For example, if an enslaver struck a person they enslaved, that person could bring their enslaver to court. Knowing what little we do about Jean, Sandwich, and colonial life there, we're left with far more questions than answers. Did Bourne choose to sell Jean because of her pregnancy or in spite of it? Did Spooner choose to buy Jean because she was pregnant, hoping she might bear a son whom he could then apprentice in the shoemaking trade? Children were often enslaved by tradesmen to be trained and apprenticed in New England. Who was her baby's father? Did Bourne or Spooner "own" other people? How did Jean come to be enslaved by Bourne? Did he travel to Boston to purchase her off the docks where people were auctioned? Was she considered a dowry from his wife's family,

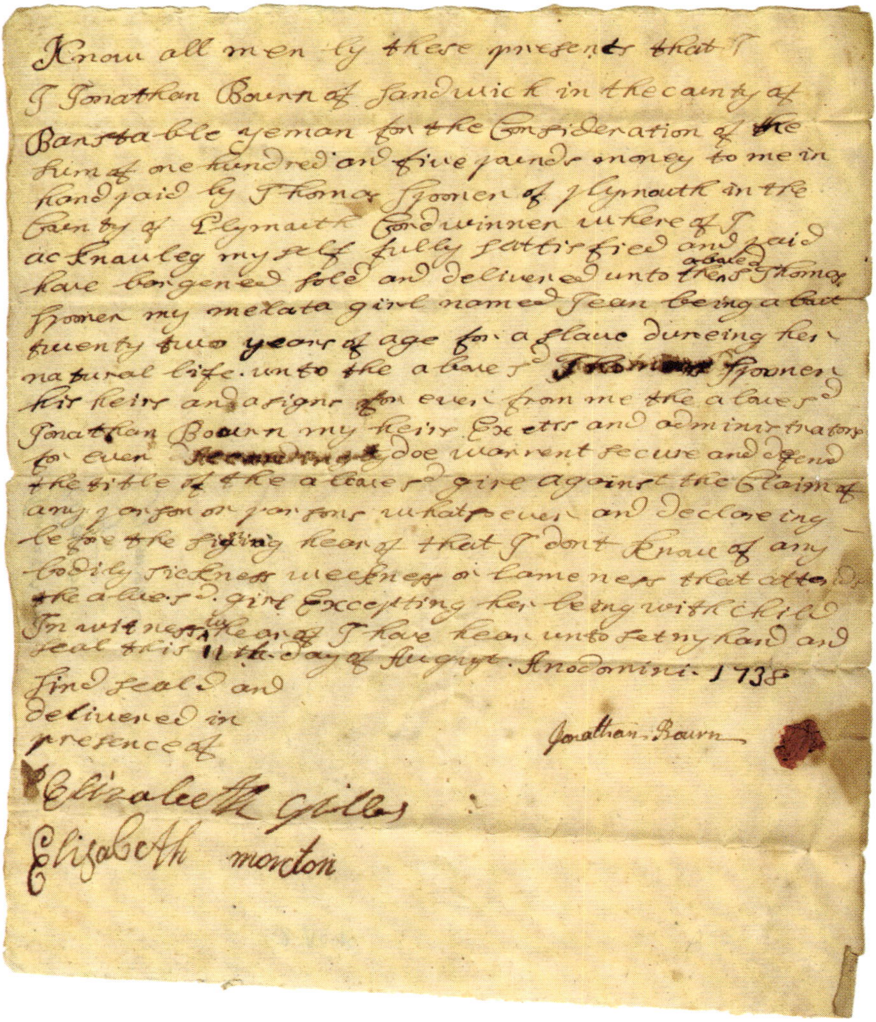
Know all men by these presents that I
I Jonathan Bourn of Sandwich in the county of
Barnstable yeman for the Consideration of the
sum of one hundred and five pounds money to me in
hand paid by Thomas Spooner of Plymouth in the
County of Plymouth Cordwinner whereof I
acknowleg myself fully sattisfied and paid
have bargained sold and delivered unto the abovesd Thomas
Spooner my molata girl named Jean being about
twenty two years of age for a slave dureing her
natural life. unto the above sd Thomas Spooner
his heirs and asigns for ever from me the above sd
Jonathan Bourn my heirs Exectrs and administrators
for ever [illegible] doe warrent secure and defend
the title of the above sd girl against the Claim of
any person or persons whatsoever and declareing
before the signing hear of that I dont know of any
bodily sickness weekness or lameness that attends
the above sd. girl Excepting her being with child
In witness whereof I have hear unto set my hand and
seal this 11th day of August. Anno domini. 1738
Signed sealed and
delivered in
presence of
Elizabeth Gilles
Elizabeth morton

Jonathan Bourn

Photo of the bill of sale between Jonathan Bourne and Thomas Spooner, transferring Jean's enslavement from one family to another. *Photo courtesy of Pilgrim Hall Museum* a gift "given"? Did Bourne inherit her? Why did he choose to "sell" her? In Jean's case, what did "mulatto" mean? Were her birth parents African and North American Indian? African and South American? African and European? What were Jean's firsts? Were her first steps here, or in Barbados, in Jamaica, in South America, on the West Coast of Africa, or the East Coast of North America? Were her first words in Spanish or creole? The language of some African nation or English or Gullah?

What we do know, standing, looking at this vast marsh, is that it's impossible to believe that Jean was unmoved by the beauty of the place and that, staring out over the ocean, she didn't long for freedom. And as we stand looking out over a view that has changed relatively little, we can know that the soft summer breezes and raging winter winds feel the same now as they did for Jean, that they come from the same corners of the earth. The rain and snow that fall are the same waters that have always rained and snowed on the shores here. All people dream and hope and long for happiness. We love and are loved. We know how these things feel.

While we don't know much about the specifics of Jean's life, we know she was here and that she was not the only woman, man, or child living a life of enslavement on Cape Cod, helping to build the communities that became this country. We owe it to them to look out over a landscape and ask questions. Perhaps, as far as firsts go, Jean is the first person enslaved on Cape Cod you've ever considered. Even if we can't find easy answers, we owe it to Jean and all the unremembered to try to find them.

A bedroom at the Benjamin Nye Homestead and Museum in Sandwich. The wallpaper uncovered on the walls around the bed shown here was verified as original to the home when it was in its oldest incarnation in 1678. Activities, lectures, and tours at the museum offer a wonderful glimpse into Cape Cod's past.
Photo by Susanna Graham-Pye

Places for Reflection
SANDWICH

SANDWICH BOARDWALK

103 Wood Avenue, Sandwich
41.76487512837636, -70.48534025926213

The beloved 1,300-foot boardwalk in Sandwich, built in the late 1800s, has taken its share of beatings from Mother Nature. While it took some time to approve, the town ultimately agreed recently to tear down and reconstruct the entire thing. While the boardwalk is not the old original, the structure offers a vantage point from which we can admire the magnificent marsh, which has always sustained the Indigenous people of the region and drew the first settlers to the area. Here, we can remember Jean and the others who lived enslaved on Cape Cod.

NYE HOUSE MUSEUM

85 Old County Road, Sandwich
41.72894688261278, -70.43143850344346

The beautiful Nye House on Old County Road offers a true step back in time. Apart from a brief period during which the state owned the home (letting it fall into disrepair), the property has been owned by the family since its construction in 1680 by Benjamin Nye. Desire Parker, in her will dated 1777, left her daughter Rebecca Nye "my negro girl called Bashua." Whether Bashua lived in the home in Sandwich or not, the house is an excellent example of the homes in which colonial residents, enslaved and enslaver alike, would have lived.

CHAPTER 2

Yarmouth–Triangle

BUT THE MINGLED, MINGLING THREADS OF LIFE ARE WOVEN BY WARP AND WOOF: CALMS CROSSED BY STORMS, A STORM FOR EVERY CALM.

—Herman Melville,

Moby Dick

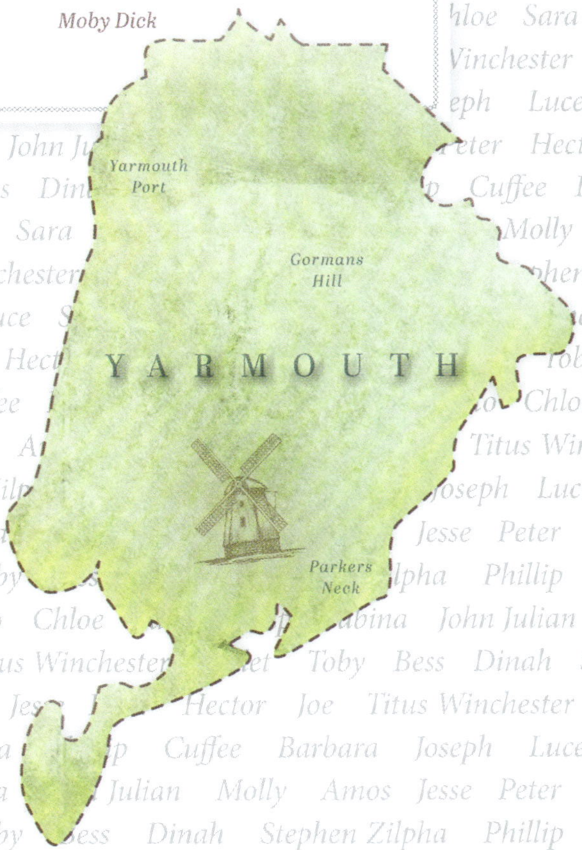

Looking north toward where the *Whydah* went down. John Julian, the ship's pilot, and all the others aboard the galley that night were likely hoping to make it to the safe port of Provincetown. The ship and crew went down off what is today Marconi Beach. *Photo by Allison Graham*

Winter tenaciously hangs on to this fragile hook of land, and spring is a time of tumultuous change. In the period between solstice and equinox, air and ocean currents collide; storms migrate, sweeping along feathered and scaly creatures of the skies and the deep. Whales and hawks, herring and hummingbirds—a spectacular host returns from wintering grounds. Rivers, knowing only one direction, carry melting snow in rushing floes of nutrients down mountains, bringing sustenance to the sea. Those who have always lived on the Cape know that spring storms can be some of the most violent—tossing up onto the beaches both life and death.

Like the people of the Cape, some red-tailed hawks stay and others migrate, coming here only for the warmer months.
Photo by Susanna Graham-Pye

Winter into spring of 1717 was no exception. A wave of weather began with one nor'easter, a kind of ocean storm fed by warmer air from the south that curls up and then spins down onto New England, often lasting for days. Like a pebble dropped in water, the storm on March 1 started a ripple that grew into a cascade. One after another, storms buried New England in a tsunami of snow. Six weeks of deep cold followed; snow drifts froze solid and locked in the colonies from Maine to Virginia. Our Jean was an infant still in March 1717, a month that came in like a lion, whipping the ocean into frothy black swells. The snow kept falling and the moonstone gray scent of sea air swept across the land. Farther inland, drifts heaped so high that some colonists in New Hampshire said they had to leave their homes by crawling from second-story windows. Livestock that had been let loose to wander starved to death.

If the weather is cold enough for long enough, even Cape Cod Bay freezes.
Photo by Allison Graham

Many people who were Indigenous in the area said they'd spoken to elderly neighbors or family members, and no one could recall winter snows like this. No lambs here; March went out like a lion too.

In early April, the *Whydah*, a square-rig, three-masted slave ship, moved up the Eastern Seaboard, traveling from the Caribbean toward Maine. As it approached the Cape, icy air lifted off the snow blanketing the land. The currents moved obediently to join the others to gather into something big and strong. The pressure was dropping, leaving everything still as the growing monster pulled energy inward, leaving only the ominous calm before the storm. In that void, a thick fog shrouded the shoreline and the future from those aboard the *Whydah Gally*.

Say "*Whydah*" today, and children—at least those from Cape Cod—say "pirate," enamored as we all seem to be, for whatever reason, with pirates. This ship, however, was named for the kingdom of Whydah, on the West Coast of Africa, located in what is today the country of Benin. More than one million people were kidnapped from their families and communities, taken away on slave ships, sold, and transported into lives of slavery from the port of Whydah. The kingdom of Whydah was the last port from which people who were meant to be enslaved were illegally exported. Today, hundreds of thousands of people have visited the Whydah Pirate Museum in Yarmouth, Cape Cod, where they can see an ever-changing variety of items constantly being recovered from what is the only authenticated "pirate ship" ever found.

The *Whydah* was commissioned in 1715 for Sir Humphrey Morris of London. Made to carry cargo, including humans, the galley ship could hold more than three hundred enslaved people. On its maiden voyage, the ship left for the western coast of Africa, carrying goods to trade for gold and people to be sold. After cruising the western coast of Africa, acquiring Akan gold and jewelry, the ship was loaded with approximately 360 captive people and headed for the Caribbean. Of that number, 312 people survived the journey known as the Middle Passage. After Captain Lawrence Prince and his crew offloaded their cargo of people, he headed home with a ship full of gold, indigo, sugar, and other treasures. In the windward passage, Captain Samuel Bellamy, a twenty-eight-year-old relatively new to the business of piracy, took the *Whydah* after a three-day chase, adding the ship to the others he'd already captured, the *Sultana* and *Mary Anne*. With his little fleet, carrying the plunder of many ships, he headed north. On the night of April 26, 1717, the *Whydah* was off Cape Cod, locked in fog. Cruising past the notorious shoals off Chatham, having agreed with his crew on the other two ships to meet in Maine, Bellamy was hit by the monster storm, taking down the *Whydah* off Wellfleet. Two out of approximately 130 men on the *Whydah* survived. The *Mary Anne* also wrecked on Pochet Island; ten—seven of whom were from Bellamy's crew—survived. The *Whydah Gally* was found in 1986, and divers have been carefully conducting an archeological recovery of the ship since.

On that night long ago, when the ship went down, an estimated one-third or more of Bellamy's crew was of African origin. Bellamy, who thought of himself as the Robin Hood of the Sea, provided freedom to those who agreed to join his crew. On board was a young boy named John Julian. A variety of sources believe that Julian met Bellamy in the Caribbean, where Bellamy had gone hunting the wreck of a fleet of Spanish ships—reputed to be carrying a fortune—that had gone down off Florida. The treasure hunting failed, but Bellamy moved on and joined the crew of pirate Benjamin Hornigold. His crew ousted Captain Hornigold and ultimately made Bellamy captain of the ship *Mary Anne*.

John Julian was born sometime in 1701 or 1702. He is described by some sources as a Miskito and by others as "part Miskito and part negro." The Mosquito Coast, named for the Miskito people, lies along the coast of what is today Nicaragua and Honduras. Very possibly John's ancestry was a blend of Central American and African. Of the estimated twelve to eighteen million people trafficked from Africa, the largest number went to Latin America. Africans bound for lives of slavery wound up on the Mosquito Coast as a result of slave ships wrecking off the coast. People who were enslaved on and escaped from sugar plantations on Caribbean islands also made their way there. In exchange for helping them establish a foothold in a region dominated by Spain, the English provided protection and weapons for the Miskito people, who also were known to participate in the capture and sale of humans.[1]

Just as people of African and European descent made their way to the Miskito coast, so too did pirates. Described as a "chokepoint along Spain's Panama–Cuba treasure route," the Miskito coast included reefs and shoals that forced ships carrying gold, silver, and jewels to slow down, allowing their capture. Pirates were known to anchor in sheltered bays along the coast, where forests provided wood for repairs, food, and fresh water. The Miskitos were described as "skilled small boat seamen [the English word "dory" comes from the Miskito *dori*] and assisted in the repairs, and worked with some of the crews as harpooners, pilots and fighters."[2] Young sixteen-year-old John's role as the pilot of the *Whydah* is not surprising, but it is unclear whether he was a slave freed by Bellamy or was a pilot on one of the ships Bellamy had captured, or if he had been free and somehow in Jamaica as someone involved in the enslavement and sale of people. Coming from the region he did, John could have come from a family of slave trackers/sellers as easily as he might have been enslaved.

While the phrase "Pirates of the Caribbean" has gained popularity in adventure stories and movies, novelty items, and childhood party themes, the "Golden Age of Piracy" in the Caribbean occurred because the islands there were the core of chattel slavery. The celebrated sea captains of New England were among the highest numbers beating down what we today call the triangular route. By the middle of the eighteenth century, the trafficking of people captured in Africa was at its height. New England shipyards churned out ships, an estimated 1,332 in the forty years between 1674 and 1714.[3] The triangular trade route currently taught in school rooms here in the United States is far simpler than the historical reality. Bellmay's course, the cargo of his ships and those he plundered, the marriages between—or forced "breeding" of—people, and the ethnic mix of people living in various stages of enslavement and sometimes, like John, freedom demonstrate this complex reality. Native people from North America, particularly northern colonies, were taken from these shores and traded for people in the Caribbean. Those people, many of African or South and Central American descent, had been taken from homes and sold onto plantations. Often, people of African descent enslaved in the Caribbean were traded for Native Americans such as the Pequot and Wampanoag because they were less likely to try to escape in unfamiliar territory. Ultimately, the so-called trian-

On the days following a storm, the ocean lies down and the air is crisp. This could have been the case as John Julian and the other survivors of the ships wrecked on that stormy spring night in 1717 tried to make their way off the Cape. *Photo by Susanna Graham-Pye*

gular trade route was less a route than an economic relationship among kingdoms in Africa, Portugal, Spain, and Great Britain and the colonies of European nations in the Americas. Central to that relationship between nations were the captains, with their crews and ships, who carried goods between markets. As the slave trade grew, the people who were Indigenous from northern colonies became less often enslaved as a punishment for crimes or as prisoners during wars and became increasingly viewed as a lucrative commodity.

Soon, trading Indigenous people for African people was replaced with trafficking people directly from Africa to North America, and Cape Cod shipmasters and seamen found growing sources of employment on the sea. In his book *History of Old Yarmouth*, Charles Francis Swift describes the early, burgeoning sea trade on Cape Cod:

> Oil, fish, and tar gathered from the forests were exchanged with the trading vessels which visited the coast, for the goods of which they stood most in need and did not produce themselves. They subsequently embarked in trade on their own account, gradually enlarging their field of enterprise. They transported their fish in their own vessels to Barbados and other West India ports, exchanged them for molasses and spirits and not only supplied their own wants but they had a surplus of trade to Boston markets.[4]

Cape mariners were integrally linked to and familiar with chattel slavery—moving food for people who were enslaved, the produce of their labors, and even the people themselves.

The seven survivors of the *Mary Anne*, as well as Thomas Davis and John from the *Whydah*, were taken from the Barnstable Jailhouse to Boston for trial. Even with that widely publicized capture and trial, details of what happened to John are scant, in all likelihood because he was not white. He was held in the Barnstable Jailhouse with Davis and the others. They were taken to Boston, where they were tried for piracy. Davis was found not guilty. The others, except John, were executed by hanging. That John was sold into slavery, perhaps to President John Adams's grandfather, is suggested in numerous writings, but there doesn't seem to be proof, nor is it clear where the notion comes from. A man known as Julian the Indian, a slave, was executed in 1733 for killing a slave hunter who was trying to capture him, and many articles, books, and stories about the *Whydah* pirates hypothesize that this may be the same John Julian who was Bellamy's pilot.

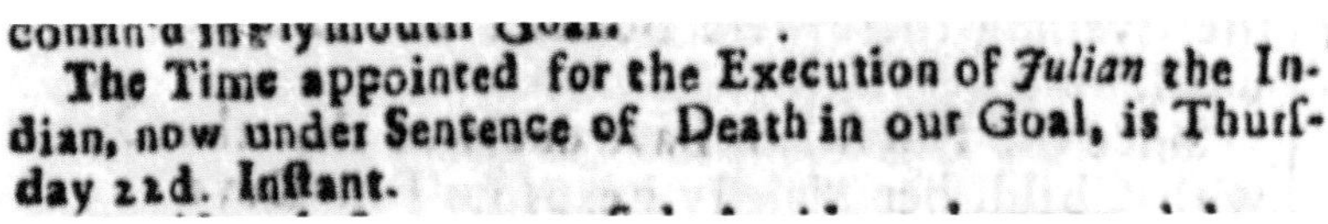

The Time appointed for the Execution of *Julian* the Indian, now under Sentence of Death in our Goal, is Thursday 22d. Instant.

A small mention of Julian the Indian's hanging. Many believe this to be the pirate John Julian, who survived the sinking of the *Whydah*.

If it were the same person, John's body after his hanging was donated to medical students for research, and his "bones were saved to make a skeleton." The *Whydah*, her cargo, her crew, and her route demonstrate why piracy flourished. That so many so-called pirates were former slaves underscores the ever-present longing for freedom found in the heart and soul of people throughout the history of enslavement.

John Julian's stay on Cape Cod was brief, as was his life, and perhaps his life of freedom. Maybe he was born free; maybe he lived free of enslavement for a brief time aboard a pirate ship bound for Maine. We can't know for sure. However, roughly thirty-seven years after the wreck of the slave ship *Whydah Gally* off the coast of Cape Cod, the town of Barnstable reported thirty-three enslaved people living there in the 1754 slave census, which was ordered by Governor William Shirley. Sixty-six years after the wreck, Massachusetts abolished slavery, the first state to do so completely. Since the ultimate fate of John Julian remains uncertain, it is nice to think that the young pilot wasn't the man who was hanged for murdering someone who wanted to return him to a life of enslavement—and that he may have even lived long enough to see abolition in Massachusetts.

Places for Reflection

YARMOUTH

TAYLOR BRAY FARM

108 Bray Farm Road, Yarmouth Port
41.72158736575764, −70.20467956111553

The Taylors of the Taylor Bray Farm were of the family into which Mercy Lord married. Mercy, whose father had given her a woman named Sabina, sold Sabina to the wealthy merchant Bourne family in Barnstable after her husband's death. The farm hosts festivals, such as its spring sheep-shearing and fall pumpkin festivals, offers tours of the farmhouse, and is open dawn to dusk. The property has walking trails as well and is a beautiful site on which to contemplate the lives of the enslaved people who lived on Cape Cod.

WHYDAH PIRATE MUSEUM

674 MA-28, West Yarmouth
41.6503248069323, −70.22500320344767

The Whydah Pirate Museum houses the largest collection of items recovered from any shipwreck in the world. It is thought to be the only authenticated pirate shipwreck. The loot recovered from the *Whydah*, a ship constructed for the purpose of trafficking people from Africa to the West Indies and other British colonized locations, offers a glimpse of the riches that were traded in exchange for the people who were enslaved and who worked to create the wealth enjoyed by many citizens of Great Britain and its colonies.

CHAPTER 3

Barnstable and Dennis—Traditions

I WONDER WHERE IS ALL MY RELATION.
FRIENDSHIP TO ALL—AND EVERY NATION.

—DAVE DRAKE,
a poet and potter who was enslaved in Old Edgefield, South Carolina. He often inscribed his pottery works with couplets.

The differences in temperature between winter and summer on Cape Cod can be extreme, ranging by as many as 90 degrees. In the winter, on ocean-deep, bone-chilling January days the temperature can hover around zero or below. On summer's hottest, humid, salty-sea days, the mercury can clear 100°F. The shoulder seasons on the Cape, because of the ocean's influence, are an odd reversal from farther inland, with the summer-warmed waters of the bay and sound moderating autumn air and the winter-frozen waters slowing spring's warmth from arriving to embrace the peninsula. The weather in South Carolina, on the other hand, is gentler. Temperatures fluctuate less and do so more languidly. Growing seasons are longer. But, north or south, weather created hardships for people enslaved throughout the English North American colonies. There were physical hardships—whether it was the radical reality of cold and snow for someone who'd been born and grew up in Barbados, or the relentless southern sun beating down on someone working in the mosquito-infested rice fields. But more than that, there were emotional hardships of being abducted from familiar environments in Africa—countries such as Congo, the region of Senegambia between the Gambia and the Senegal Rivers, or Angola—and taken to a new world an ocean away.

Angolan woman, depicted here in traditional dress. Many women who were enslaved in Barbados and what became South Carolina were of Angolan descent. Cultural aspects of life, including patterns used when weaving and methods of making baskets used for daily chores, were better preserved where entire communities of people who were enslaved lived together. In New England, there were far fewer people enslaved; hence less chance to keep traditions alive.

In the Cape Cod town of Dennis, part of which later became Yarmouth, a woman named Sabina lived with Mercy and Shubael Taylor and their children. Mercy said Sabina was "given" to her by her father, the Reverend Joseph Lord, "before my wedding."[1] Whether this means Sabina was considered to belong to Mercy prior to her wedding or if Sabina was a gift upon Mercy's marriage to Shubael is difficult to discern, as is so much of Sabina's life and the lives of thousands of those in the Northeast who were forced down a path none would have chosen.

While the smallest details of colonial people's lives can, with enough persistence, be tracked down, finding information about the people who were enslaved is difficult, if not impossible. The little that can be found about Sabina, within the context of the well-established and recorded lives of her enslavers, provides a structure to look at her life and the larger picture of the lives of enslaved people in New England, and more specifically Cape Cod.

Sabina lived in many of the settings a woman enslaved in New England might: the three families we know that enslaved Sabina over the course of her life—the Lord family, the Taylor home, and the Bourn (also spelled Bourne) family—represent three strata in the societal structure of colonial New England. Sabina likely lived enslaved first in the South, then in the North, so her experiences also represent a broader colonial view.

Mercy Lord Taylor's father, Reverend Joseph Lord, was born in Charlestown in Massachusetts Bay Colony. Lord married Abigail Hinckley, the daughter of Governor Thomas Hinckley. Lord attended Harvard and was ordained as a Puritan minister in Dorchester, Massachusetts. Soon after, he was "sent forth" from that church to build a church in South Carolina, which he did and around which was built a new settlement: Dorchester, South Carolina. Built on the banks of the Ashley River, roughly 45 miles from Charlestown (later renamed Charleston), not only was the small community there a mission to bring the Congregational Puritan church to the South, but those who moved there also hoped to make lives for themselves and, perhaps, prosper. Rice was the main crop being grown.

Joseph and Abigail had eight children; Mercy was their oldest, born in 1698 or 1699 in Dorchester, South Carolina. Lord traveled back and forth between Massachusetts and South Carolina, and numerous records say that, at some point, Mercy came back with her father and stayed in Dorchester, Massachusetts. If this is true, Reverend Lord might have given Sabina to Mercy when his daughter opted to live apart from the rest of the family in the North. Lord left South Carolina and came to Chatham, where he firmly established the fledgling First Congregational Church. Mercy married

Shubael Taylor of Yarmouth in September 1729. The couple had five children. Shubael, a deacon of his church, died in 1762.

These are the facts. Using these facts like an armature, piecing onto it bits of detail like clay, we can create a possible image of Sabina. If the story is not 100 percent accurate for Sabina, hers certainly represents many people's lives and the factual realities that shaped them.

Very likely, Sabina came north from South Carolina. In the bill of sale to the Bournes, Mercy describes Sabina as "supposed to be part negro born of a Spanish Indian woman slave or sarvant for life then to my honored father." While it appears that Sabina's father was likely African, her mother's ethnicity could be rooted in several scenarios. Whatever Sabina's mother's ancestry, the presence of a Spanish Indian woman—one in a relationship with a "negro," as Sabina's father is called—was more likely in South Carolina than Massachusetts. The Lords lived in South Carolina for twenty years, coming to Chatham in 1720. Mercy was married in 1729, and Sabina had been enslaved by Joseph Lord, Mercy's father, prior to that year.

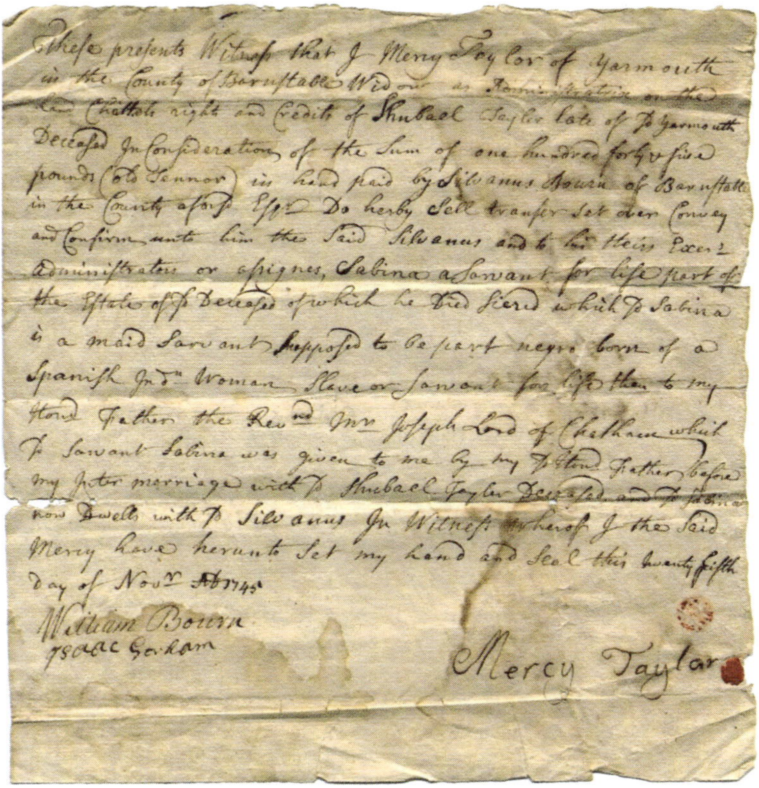
These presents Witness that I Mercy Taylor of Yarmouth in the County of Barnstable Widow as Administratrix on the Chattels rights and Credits of Shubael Taylor late of sd Yarmouth Deceased In Consideration of the Sum of one hundred forty five pounds (old Tennor) in hand paid by Silvanus Bourn of Barnstable in the County afores[d] Esq Do hereby Sell transfer Set over Convey and Confirm unto him the Said Silvanus and to his Heirs Execr[s] Administrators or assignes, Sabina a Servant for life part of the Estate of sd Deceased of which he Died Seized which sd Sabina is a maid Servant Supposed to be part negro born of a Spanish Ind[n] Woman Slave or Servant for life then to my Hond Father the Rev[d] Mr Joseph Lord of Chatham which sd Servant Sabina was given to me by my sd Hond Father before my former marriage with sd Shubael Taylor Deceased and sd Sabina now Dwells with sd Silvanus In Witness whereof I the Said Mercy have hereunto Set my hand and Seal this twenty fifth day of Nov[r] 1745

William Bourn
Isaac Gorham

Mercy Taylor

Bill of sale for Sabina from Mercy Taylor to Sylvanus Bourne.
Courtesy of Dennis Historical Society

When the Lord family first went to Carolina Colony, it had not yet been divided into north and south. The colony received its charter from King Charles II of England in 1663 and was a direct offshoot of the colony of Barbados, the earliest settlers coming from that island to the North American coastal colony. While sugar was the main commodity produced in the Barbados system, where people of African descent outnumbered their white European enslavers ten to one, Carolina's primary crops were rice and indigo. Modeled on Barbados's constitution, the Fundamental Constitution of Carolina had a strict slave code that unambiguously defined and enforced the enslavement of people who were called chattel property (Barbadian laws defined people who were enslaved as "real estate"). Whether or not Lord and his collection of colonists were enticed by this offer, settlers in Carolina were offered 20 acres of land for every male defined as "negro" whom they enslaved; 10 acres for every woman "negro."

During the late seventeenth and early eighteenth centuries, when the Lord family lived in Carolina, between one-third to one-half of people who were enslaved in the young colony came from the English West Indies.[2] Could Sabina's mother have come from there? Possibly. While records indicate Native communities of people on Barbados during the early sixteenth century, those populations were nearly completely wiped out after the islands of the region had been raided by Spain for people to work in the mines of Hispaniola. When the island became the focus of England's colonization efforts, a small group of people from the Arawak tribe of Guiana were brought to the island to help settlers understand how to grow crops there. The history of those people and their relationship with the people developing a plantation system in Barbados is relatively short but complicated. Ultimately, it boiled down to the fact that the people who had come to help the colonists were in turn enslaved.

The enslavement of the Arawaks set a precedent for the enslavement of other Native people from surrounding areas. Richard Ligon, who wrote *True and Exact History of the Island of Barbados*, first published in 1657, describes the presence of Native South American Indians "fetched from other countries; some from neighboring islands, some from the Main, which we make slaves."[3] Following this tangled thread could connect Sabina and her mother to Barbados, with its deep ties to Carolina, and South American Indian ancestry.

Another scenario for Sabina's family of origin could be that she was born in South Carolina. That she was kidnapped and trafficked directly from an African country seems unlikely with the reference to her South American Indian mother.

A print of a woman shown in South Carolina. The image, printed in the *Illustrated London News*, shows the woman surrounded by children of both European and African descent. Sabina's role, or even her presence, with the Lord family in what was then simply called Carolina, would have included caring for children in the growing Lord family.

The Ashley River, along the banks of which Lord built his church, is described today as "the Black Pearl" of South Carolina. It wends its way from a cypress swamp down into the salt marshes of the low country. For people taken from their homes in certain regions of West Africa, the landscape and climate were similar to what they'd known at home. Many of the people brought to Carolina were chosen and enslaved from communities in Africa specifically known for their cultivation of rice. Enslavers referred to the region of West Africa along the coast, from Senegal to Sierra Leone and Liberia, as the Rice Coast. People from this region were, according to some sources, the largest group brought to South Carolina and Georgia. Songs, language, and stories from that part of Africa were preserved then as they continue to be today among the Gullah people. Sabina's father could have been one of these people. One thing is certain: in South Carolina, Sabina would have lived in the presence of many people like her. So many people being enslaved by South Carolinians allowed for a kind of community where cultural traditions from communities in Africa and Barbados were kept alive and shared, creating bonds and connections for people from whom so much had been stolen. At least there, Sabina would have had a sense of belonging.

This painting, one of the most well known of people living in this area in enslavement, was created sometime between 1785 and 1795. It illustrates people who were enslaved in South Carolina in the eighteenth century. That larger numbers of people of African descent lived in southern colonies allowed for the preservation and creation of culture and community. The painting is housed today in Colonial Williamsburg, Virginia. *Courtesy of the Colonial Williamsburg Foundation*

In the areas of Africa from which people were trafficked, most religions were polytheistic. Many West African religions worshiped one supreme god and lesser gods. Much like early Judaism, prayer and sacrifice were aspects of religious rituals. Music and dance were also significant. In areas such as the Carolinas, the level of the preservation of traditions from countries in Africa went hand in hand with the density of the African populations.

Baskets, woven using a traditional coil method, were made; songs and language were preserved, calls and responses were chanted, and stories were told; banjos were made from gourds; healing rituals and actions of faith rooted in a different daily life were practiced; and all survived due to a population large enough to form a community that could preserve tradition and culture. And, as was true for other polytheistic communities, accepting an additional god, such as a Christian god, was possible. How different the world must have felt for Sabina upon the Lords' return to Massachusetts.

In 1718 (dates vary between 1717 and 1720), Lord came to Chatham, newly incorporated, to help build a congregation and church. Whether the Lords' first winter in Chatham was in 1717, the winter of the Great Snow, the spring of the nor'easter that sank the *Whydah*, or during a more typical, bleak season, it would have been traumatic for someone who'd lived in South Carolina, the coastal region of Africa, or the West Indies for all her life. Had Sabina ever seen snow? Had she ever felt temperatures as low as they fall during a Cape Cod winter? The home built for the Lords, "just west of the old cemeteries," was relatively isolated. The lives of people who were enslaved in Massachusetts, in this case on Cape Cod, were far different from the lives of the people in South Carolina, and the sense of loneliness for Sabina, emotionally and physically, must have been extreme.

At the time of the Lords' departure from Carolina, the population of people of African ancestry outnumbered people who were white. Of the estimated 18,000 people living there, the number of enslaved people is thought to have been 65 to 70 percent of the population. Upon the family's return to Massachusetts, estimates of the number of people who were identified as "black" or "negro" hover between three thousand and four thousand, with approximately two thousand of those people enslaved. In communities with larger ports and greater wealth, such as Boston, more people enslaved greater numbers of people, allowing for a sense of shared community in a larger population of people of color. Households, such as the Royalls of Medford, who enslaved more than sixty people, had a larger number of people enslaved. On Cape Cod, however, homes were far apart, and families for the most part might enslave one or two people, if any at all. Sabina and the others who likely had little opportunity to socialize with other people with a shared heritage must have been lonely. Cape Cod's culture was grounded in a predominantly Puritan culture that dominated all aspects of life. Living in a minister's home, Sabina would have been expected to live as the Lords did.

When Mercy married Shubael Taylor, another phase of Sabina's life began in Yarmouth. Sabina was no longer living in the plantation world of the South or the home of a minister in Chatham, and her work would have been helping Mercy raise her children and care for the family's home. Author Charles Francis Swift describes early life in Yarmouth in one of his books:

> The early business pursuits of the settlers were, as has been seen, agriculture, stock raising and the fisheries. Whales were cast upon the coast, and the citizens had many a sharp controversy with the government which claimed these waifs of the sea as its rightful perquisite. Oil, fish, and tar gathered from the forests, were exchanged with the trading vessels which visited the coast, for the goods of which they stood most in need and did not produce themselves. They subsequently embarked in trade on their own account, gradually enlarging their field of enterprise. They transported their fish in their own vessels to Barbados and other West India ports, exchanged them for molasses and spirits and not only supplied their own wants but they had a surplus of trade to Boston markets.[4]

The book describes crops, which included Indian corn, rye, barley, and wheat, as well as vegetables and fruits. Orchards offered apples, Kentish cherries, peaches, and pear trees. There was a fulling mill on western Swan Pond River. Women, Swift explains, were "expert and skillful in the use of the loom and made most of the cloth of their households. . . .

Goats were sometimes kept by people in colonial days. Goats and other livestock can be seen at Taylor Bray Farm in Yarmouth. The Taylors associated with this property were Shubael's family. No records found connected Mercy Lord Taylor and her husband to use of this spot. However, the farm complex provides a beautiful example of homesites and farms in the area during the colonial and postrevolutionary eras. The town purchased the property for conservation in the 1980s, and the Taylor Bray Preservation Association works to maintain the complex. In addition to donated labor, volunteers run or host festivals and educational lectures and classes. The association's website keeps a calendar of events. *Photo by Susanna Graham-Pye*

Tables were abundantly supplied with game and fish and products of their fields. Cattle soon became plentiful—goats were kept for milk and bees for honey. . . . Beer was regarded as a prime necessity and each family brewing at regular intervals."

After Shubael's death, Mercy sold Sabina to Sylvanus Bourne, and another new chapter began for Sabina in Barnstable in what was likely yet another kind of colonial life. The Bournes were a prominent family in town. Sylvanus was a wealthy merchant and lawyer. A portrait of his wife, Mercy

The last known home for Sabina was with the Bourne family of Barnstable. Mercy Bourne, shown here in a painting by John Singleton Copley, mentions in her will the people she enslaved, but Sabina's name is not among them. Mercy is shown here holding a Common Book of Prayer, a symbol that she was a member of the Church of England. The oil-on-canvas painting is at the Metropolitan Museum of Art in New York. *Courtesy of the Morris K. Jesup Fund, 1924*

Bourne, painted by artist John Singleton Copley shows the elderly woman holding an English prayer book, indicating her affiliation with the Episcopal Church. Mercy was known to have a taste for good wine and may have been an innovator of sorts, "manufacturing for her house a peculiar wool shirting."[5] The Bournes probably celebrated holidays, such as Christmas, with more pomp than would have been observed in an austere pastor's or deacon's home.

In the Bourne household, Sabina would have lived with other people who were enslaved; both Silvanus's and Mercy's wills included provisions for them. Mercy outlived her husband, and when she passed away in 1782, she left her son Richard—among other possessions—"My negro boy Cato, provided at 35 he manumit him with sufficient security under the law." "Negro girl Chloe" was allowed to choose which of Mercy's surviving children she wished to live with, provided this child paid the executor of the will "so much as she is valued at by indifferent men appointed for that purpose."[6]

There is no mention of Sabina. Depending on her age at the Lord family's arrival in 1720, Sabina could have passed away years before her enslavers did, leaving only a faint trail upon which we can travel as we try to understand the life she was forced to live.

Places for Reflection

BARNSTABLE & DENNIS

THE OLD JAILHOUSE

3353 Route 6A, Barnstable
41.70026518710237, -70.29856254207093

The Old Jailhouse, built in 1690 by order of the authorities of Plymouth and Massachusetts Bay Colonies, served as Barnstable County's jail for more than a hundred years and is reputed to be the oldest surviving wooden colonial-era jailhouse in the country. John Julian and the other survivors of the Whydah shipwreck were held there until they were moved to Boston for trial. A Brewster woman who was enslaved by a Cape family was also imprisoned there because she was found beside the body of her lifeless infant. She was imprisoned in the jailhouse to await trial for murder but was found to be innocent of the crime.

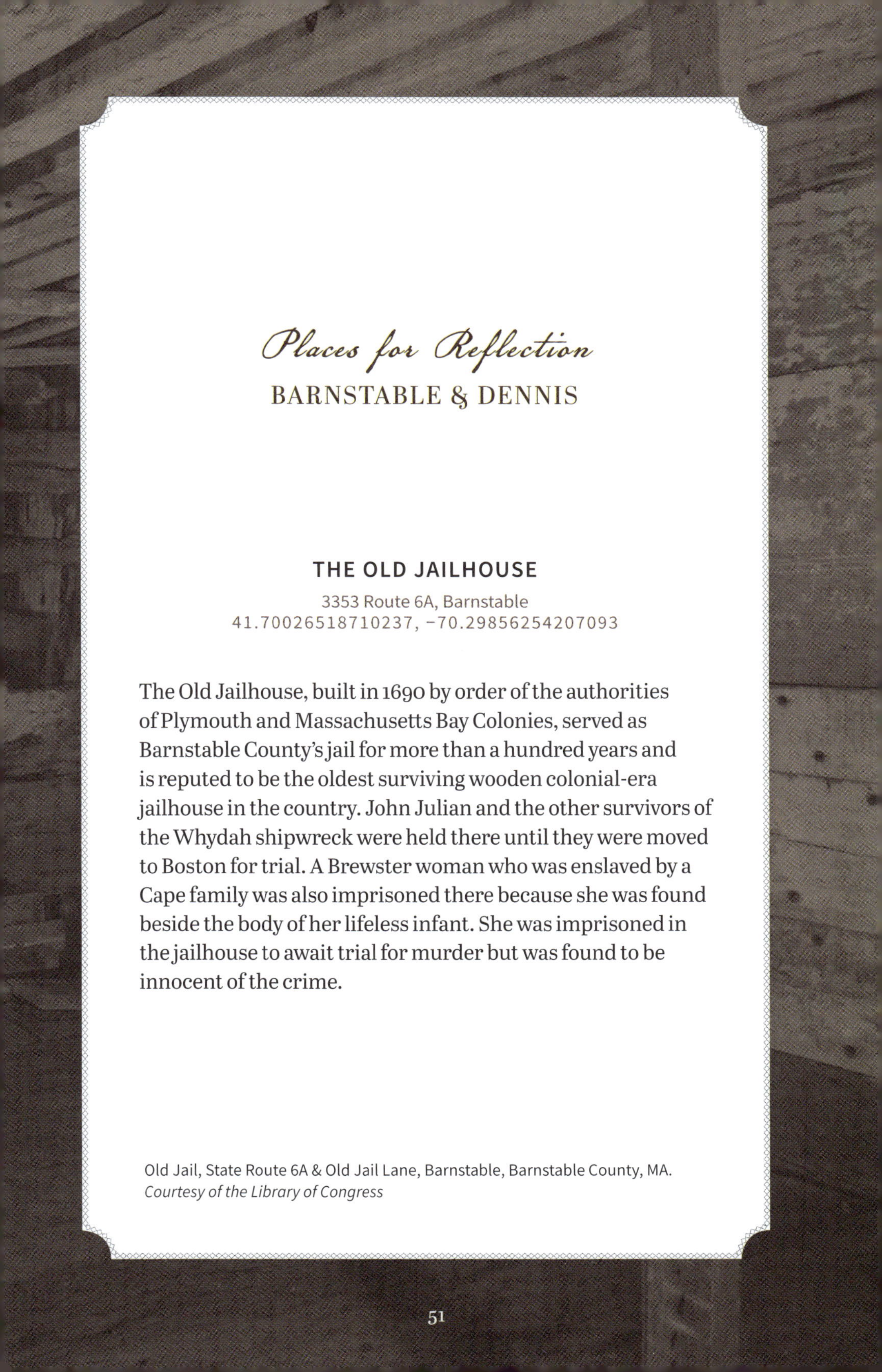

Old Jail, State Route 6A & Old Jail Lane, Barnstable, Barnstable County, MA.
Courtesy of the Library of Congress

CHAPTER 4

Eastham—Encounters and Economics

I, young in life, by seeming cruel fate
Was snatch'd from Afric's fancy'd happy seat:
What pangs excruciating must molest,
What sorrows labour in my parent's breast?
Steel'd was that soul and by no misery mov'd
That from a father seiz'd his babe belov'd:
Such, such my case. And can I then but pray
Others may never feel tyrannic sway?

—Phillis Wheatley Peters

At First Encounter Beach, the dark angles of the beach plum bushes stand with their bare winter branches in silhouette against the frozen hard sand dunes. Their shapes, craggy and angled and sharp, with sudden changes in direction, are an apt visual representation of life here on this part of the Cape and the history of Cape Cod in general, and a reflection of our history as a nation. Like the seasons full of storms and sun, droughts, and rains and snows that have shaped the old bushes, the changes in philosophies, assumptions, laws, and rights in this country have had an effect on our history and our view of it over time.

First Encounter is so named for the meeting between the Native people of the area and the Pilgrims of the *Mayflower*. But before anyone could even get off the ship, those in charge of the small band of people who'd traveled across the Atlantic, missing their mark of Virginia, were required to sign the Mayflower Compact. Those who stand on the beach today and look out to the horizon over Cape Cod Bay can see the tides pull the waters back, letting them seem to slip over the edge of the earth, before they're pulled

when he asks that his heirs make to "put them in a way that they may not want." The use of "they," the hope they wanted for nothing, somehow evokes the image of a couple.

People gather along the shores of Cape Cod Bay to watch the sunset. *Photo by Zukhra Graham*

Freeman was born in Sussex, England. He had arrived in Lynn, Massachusetts Bay Colony, as a child and moved to Sandwich with his parents and siblings. He fought in King Philip's War and was a surveyor, a deacon, a selectman, a judge, and a major. Letters and lofty histories written in genealogies over the years celebrate his accomplishments. But what of Toby and Bess? They, like Freeman, very likely traveled across the Atlantic Ocean, but their journey was forced. They, like Freeman, worked to build a lasting settlement that grew into the town of Eastham. Did Toby travel with Freeman when he fought in the war? Or did he stay home to work, herding sheep and cattle and harvesting food for Freeman's family and animals? Did Bess help raise the children who went on to grow up and to whom Freeman left large tracts of land and sums of money? Toby and Bess seem to be Eastham's only people who were enslaved, or at least the only ones for whom records can be found. They were here. We know this.

In her work *Documents Illustrative of the Slave Trade in America*, Elizabeth Donnan wrote, "At the opening of the eighteenth century the African slave trade was the foundation on which colonial industry and the colonial commerce of European countries rested."[4] She goes on to say that the commercial trade of humans dominated the relationship between western European nations and their colonies. Major John Freeman was considered a wealthy, successful man, and upon his death he asked that his sons manumit those who had worked alongside him to make him that.

Freeman died just shy of one hundred years after the so-called First Encounter with the people who were native to the area, people who called their home Nauset, which means the "Place Between." The name seems a poignant harbinger, since the people whose ancestors had been here for thousands of years encountered those who'd just arrived and whose successes would depend on exporting people who were Natives and importing people from another continent for enslavement.

Places for Reflection

EASTHAM

FIRST ENCOUNTER BEACH

Located on the bayside of Eastham
41.82274294435156, -70.00396257051797

A plaque at First Encounter Beach was erected in 2001, reading "Near this site, the Nauset Tribe of the Wampanoag Nation, seeking to protect themselves and their culture had their first encounter with Miles Standish, John Carver, William Bradford, Edward Winslow, John Tilly," and a host of others' names. An attempt to more accurately reflect the reality of that initial meeting, this plaque was meant to soften the content of the one erected in 1920 to commemorate the three hundredth anniversary of the First Encounter. That monument, tucked away in the dunes at the beach, reads "On this spot hostile Indians had their first encounter, Dec. 8, 1620."

INDIAN ROCK ON THE FORT HILL TRAIL

Fort Hill Road off US 6, Eastham
41.8191162769619, -69.96467813227454

Along the Cape Cod National Seashore trail that runs between Fort Hill and Skiff Hill, a 20-ton granitic glacial boulder, once used by Native Americans for tool sharpening, sits atop a bluff overlooking Nauset Marsh. The boulder originally sat on the marsh just south of Hemenway Landing. As the ever-shifting ocean and barrier marsh moved farther inland, the boulder nearly disappeared. It was moved to the top of Skiff Hill, and the original site is underwater. The stone was probably used for sharpening bone items such as harpoon heads, fishhooks, and stone axes and is a reminder of the large population of people who lived and worked here prior to colonists' arrival.

CHAPTER 5

Brewster—Captains

ITS STREETS WERE SHADED WITH FINE OLD TREES, ITS HOUSES WERE LARGE AND SUBSTANTIAL AND THE MEN WHO BUILT AND OWNED THEM WERE LARGE AND SUBSTANTIAL, TOO. THEY MADE THEIR FORTUNES—FORTUNES THAT WERE THE BEGINNINGS OF BIGGER ONES FOR THEIR DESCENDANTS IN BOSTON, NEW YORK AND MANY ANOTHER CITY—BY SAILING OVER PRETTY NEARLY ALL THE WET PLACES ON THE EARTH'S SURFACE AND BARGAINING AND RISKING AND DARING, WITH YANKEE SHREWDNESS AND YANKEE BRAVERY.

—JOSEPH LINCOLN

Route 6A, also known as the King's Highway, is one of the oldest roads on Cape Cod and stretches nearly the entire length of the peninsula. In Brewster, antique homes, many of which were built by the town's sea captains, line the way. Pictured here, just off Route 6A, is the Captain Elijah Cobb House, home today to the Brewster Historical Society. *Photo by Susanna Graham-Pye*

Sea captains' homes line streets in old neighborhoods across the Cape. With Thanksgiving come and gone, a drive down Route 6A, the Old King's Highway, in early December is a feast for the eye. Garlands and swags of fragrant evergreens decorate tastefully restored homes. White Christmas lights sparkle from windows, casting pools of gold into the snowy darkness. Built during different periods of this narrow land's more recent history, the homes represent a timeline of sorts, each as unique and lovely as favorite Christmas ornaments. Called Saquatucket by the people who are native to the area, Brewster by its European settlers, the town claims to be "the Sea Captains' Town," a boast made in different ways by different towns, each with a history of resident captains who put Cape Cod on the map of the times. Harwich and Dennis share "Captain's Row"; Yarmouth has "Captain's Mile." No more or less than other towns, Brewster holds its rightful spot high on the list of places where scores of seamen lived—among them captains and shipmasters who, during the seventeenth through the nineteenth centuries, oversaw the movement of the commodities bought and sold around the globe.

Captain J. Henry Sears, of Brewster, was born in 1829. He lived a long life, dying at age eighty-three, and might be called the captain of Brewster's captains. In his book, *Brewster Ship Masters*, he chronicled the lives of the town's mariners—gathering them together onto the pages of his book as a good captain gathers the crew on the deck of the ship. The book captures more than the biographies of the town's notable seamen, showing the transition of the men and their work through colonial developments and milestones such as the Civil War, the abolition of slavery, and the integral role of New Englanders in the successes and failures surrounding those historic events. He points out that "most of the young men in the town who followed the sea became masters of vessels engaged with trade to all parts of the world."[1] Traveling the globe, these men (and occasionally women) saw exotic, far-flung places and brought home beautiful treasures and ideas of what a grand home should be. Mariners across the Cape planted unique plants and trees for the well-tended properties surrounding their elegant homes. Today these architectural antiques imbue the area with a sense of history and charm, but they also create an understanding of the massive wealth made in maritime trading.

Glaringly absent from our romantic recollections of bygone seafaring days are the people who, one way or another, made this wealth possible: the people who labored in the South and in the West Indies in brutal conditions to grow the sugar that created the molasses that created the rum that was traded for people. The people who, after being kidnapped, trafficked, and enslaved, also grew rice, indigo, and cotton that were traded for more people kidnapped from their homes, families, and cultures and shipped to the West Indies and Americas. Between 1768 and 1772, Massachusetts imported 8.2 million gallons of molasses. Molasses, a byproduct of sugar production, is the key ingredient in rum production. Boston became one of the leading producers of rum in the eighteenth-century world. Rum was shipped to West Africa and traded for people who were then forced to the West Indies to work on the sugar plantations. This truly vicious cycle required talented mariners to captain the boats that moved all of this—enslaved people and goods—around the world.

Some argue it was from the port of Boston that a trade route was born. What began with the first shipment of people who'd been abducted from Africa was eventually beaten down by New England ships into the pattern known as the triangular trade route. Between 1678 and 1807, as many as 45,000 people were trafficked from Africa in at least 314 voyages that landed in New England. Between 1645 and 1860, thousands of voyages left New England and traveled the triangle, transporting thousands of

A sugar loaf and sugar nips at the Nye Homestead and Museum in Sandwich. Sugar was shipped and purchased in these loaves; chunks were snipped off to sweeten food and tea. It is difficult to contemplate how much life, culture, and humanity were lost in the production of sugar.
Photo by Susanna Graham-Pye

people between African countries, the West Indies, and North American colonies.[2] Even if specific shipmasters weren't involved directly with trafficking people, the Cape's production of salt, its fisheries, and shipbuilding supported enslavement. New England shipmasters participated illicitly in trafficking people even after the importation of people from other countries for the purpose of enslaving them was made illegal by Congress in 1807. People from New England bought shares in transatlantic voyages that involved trafficking humans. Explicitly or implicitly, Cape Cod's successes and survival were entangled with slavery.

None of the Cape homes in which people who were enslaved lived compares to the Royall house of Medford, Massachusetts. The Royall family made its great wealth by trading rum and sugar—and by trafficking people. The family owned a sugar plantation in Antigua and enslaved the highest number of people of any family in the Northeast during colonial times, with as many as sixty people living in enslavement on a 10-acre property outside Boston. Nevertheless, many of the homes of sea captains on Cape Cod were grand in comparison to the typical, simple Cape favored by early Europeans who settled the peninsula. Under a number of the roofs of Brewster's homes, and others around the Cape, people who were enslavers and who were enslaved lived side by side.

Calling Massachusetts's merchants "the most vigorous slave traders in the world," A. Leon Higginbotham, a federal court justice, civil rights activist, and legal historian, once pointed out that these merchants made "enormous profits."[3] Those profits are reflected in Brewster's beautiful captains' homes. Sandwiched between the major ports of Boston and Rhode Island, Cape Cod was renowned as a nursery for the seamen of New England. Generations of shipmasters born on the Cape went to work for themselves or other regional shipping companies. Sears said, "It is believed that more shipmasters engaged in foreign trade went from the town of Brewster than from any other town or place in the country, in numerical proportion to its inhabitants." He goes on to say that "most of the young men in the town who followed the sea became masters of vessels engaged with trade to all parts of the world."[4]

These captains witnessed human trafficking of all forms around the globe. Captain Austin Bearse, of Barnstable, who describes in his book the slavery he saw in other countries, concluded that "American slavery . . . the internal slave trade, as I have seen it on the rice and sugar plantations, and in the city of New Orleans, was full as bad as any slavery in the world."

Not only were those who made their livings on the water witness to the enslavement and brutal forced labor of people, they participated in it. In *Reminiscences of Fugitive Slave Law Days in Boston*, Bearse wrote,

> It is well known that many New England vessels are in the habit of spending their winters on the Southern coast, in pursuit of this business—for vessels used to run up the rivers for the rough rice and cotton of the plantations, which we took to Charleston. We often carried gangs of slaves to the plantations as they had been ordered. These slaves were generally collected by slave-traders in Charleston, brought there by various causes such as the death of owners and the division of estates. . . . In my past days, the system of slavery was not much discussed. I saw these things as others did, without interference."[5]

The springtime sparkling water of Stony Brook, free from ice, heralds spring. *Photos by Susanna Graham-Pye*

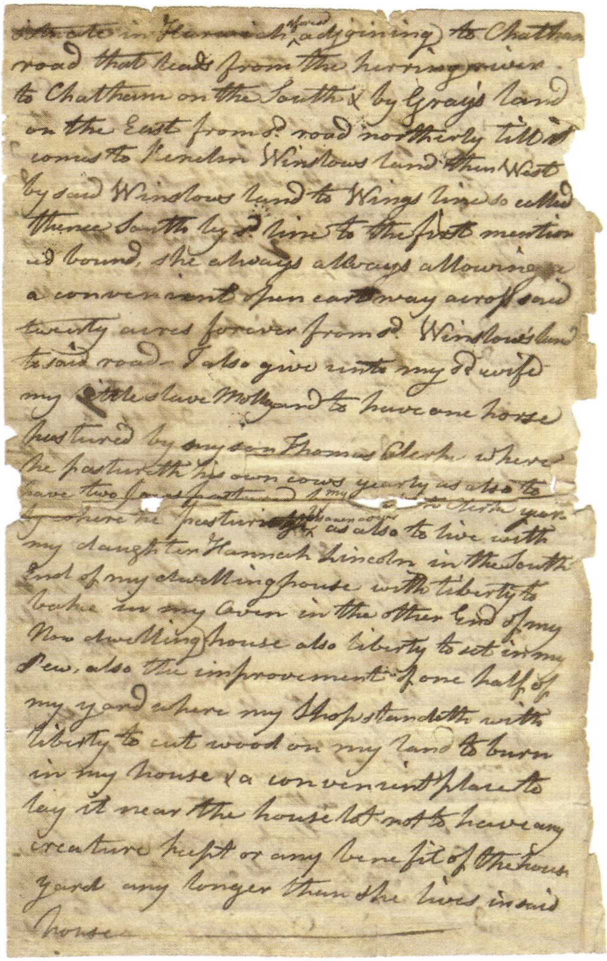

situate in Harwich and adjoining to Chatham
road that leads from the herring river
to Chatham on the South & by Gray's land
on the East from sd road northerly till it
comes to Kenelm Winslows land then West
by said Winslows land to Wings line so called
thence South by sd line to the first mention
ed bound, she always allways allowing
a convenient open cartway across said
twenty acres forever from sd Winslow's land
to said road. I also give unto my sd wife
my little slave Molly and to have one horse
pastured by my son Thomas Clark where
he pastureth his own cows yearly as also to
have two [illegible]
[illegible] where he pastureth [illegible] as also to live with
my daughter Hannah Lincoln in the South
End of my dwelling house with liberty to
bake in my Oven in the other End of my
Now dwelling house also liberty to set in my
Pew, also the improvement of one half of
my yard where my shop standeth with
liberty to cut wood on my land to burn
in my house & a convenient place to
lay it near the house but not to have any
creature kept or any benefit of the house
yard any longer than she lives in said
house

Perhaps "little Molly," enslaved by Thomas Clark, played along the banks of the Stony Brook.

Before the sea captains of Brewster and the other towns of Cape Cod traveled the world's oceans, residents focused on building sustainable communities. One of the first enterprises the town tackled was the construction of a gristmill. In 1663, Thomas Prence purchased land on Stony Brook from the native people of the area. He built the gristmill. Thomas Clark of Plymouth purchased the mill in 1677, and the mill was operated by the Clark family for several generations. In his will, Thomas Clark, the grandson named for his grandfather who purchased the mill, gives "little Molly" to his wife. The simple adjective written before her name gives nuance to our imaginings, something to grasp at as we try to know people unremembered. Was she a child? Was she petite? Was the adjective, perhaps, a term of endearment?

Bookstores across the region today have shelves devoted to the lives of the sea captains who called Cape Cod home. Streets are named for them—Freeman's Way, Linnell Road, Crowell Road, Bearse's Way—as are beaches such as Crosby and Linnell Landings, and even golf course holes. Inns and restaurants, old and new, bear the names of these seafarers. But what of "little negro Molly," whom Clark left to his wife? What of Sarah, Jesse, Hannah, Oliver, Jolly, Jack, Hamsheir, James, and Millie? These are the known names of people who were enslaved in Brewster by townspeople. Their names are recorded only on the pages of wills and in bills of sale. Thomas Clark's second wife, Patience, was bequeathed an "old negro man" and a "negro girl." In a time when women could not own any property, was the "negro girl" little Molly? Was she a possession that came to the marriage with Patience to be bequeathed back to her upon Clark's death?

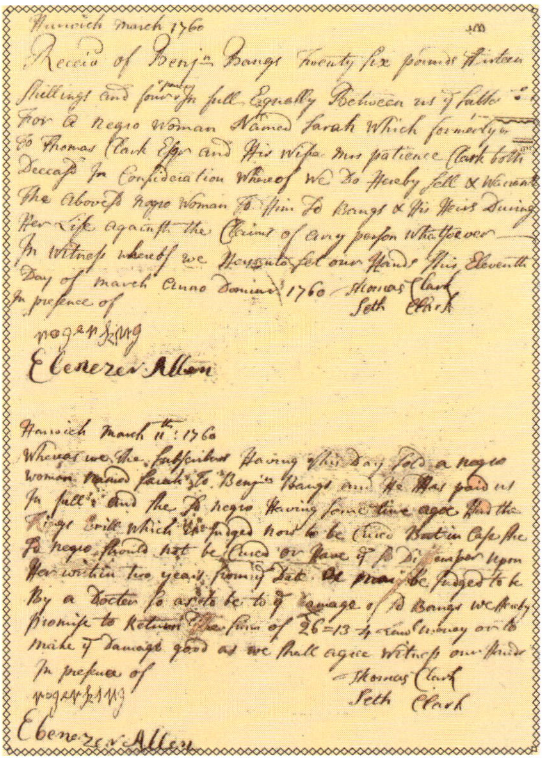
Harwich March 1760

Receiv'd of Benjn Bangs Twenty six pounds Thirteen Shillings and four pence in full Equally Between us y^e Sellers For a Negro Woman Named Sarah Which formerly [illegible] to Thomas Clark Esqr and His Wife Mrs Patience Clark both Deceas'd In Consideration Whereof We Do Hereby Sell & Warrant The aboves^d Negro Woman To Him Ye Bangs & His Heirs During Her Life against the Claims of any person Whatsoever — In Witness whereof we Hereunto Set our Hands This Eleventh Day of March Anno Domini 1760

Thomas Clark
Seth Clark

In presence of
[illegible]
Ebenezer Allen

Harwich March 11th: 1760

Whereas we the Subscribers Having this Day Sold a Negro Woman Named Sarah To Benjn Bangs and He Has paid us In full & and the S^d Negro Having some time agoe Had the Kings Evill which Is Judged now to be Cured But in Case the S^d Negro should not be Cured or have y^e S^d Distemper upon Her within two years from y^e Date [illegible] be Judged to be By a Doctor So as to be to y^e Damage of S^d Bangs We Hereby promise to Return the Sum of 26=13=4 Lawfull Money or to make y^e Damage good as we shall agree Witness our Hands

In presence of
[illegible]
Ebenezer Allen

Thomas Clark
Seth Clark

A bill of sale for Sarah.
Photo courtesy of Brewster Historical Society

Benjamin Bangs, a whaler and prominent merchant, sold "Negro Oliver" for £39; another bill of sale from Bangs shows the sale of Sarah for £25, with the provision that the sum would be returned if Sarah was found to have tuberculosis. John Freeman, enslaver of Hamsheir, signed the covenant that formed the First Parish Church of Brewster. Bangs lived across from that church. His diary includes the aforementioned purchase of Sarah; a "Silas Negro," who was given to him; and "Negro Oliver," whom he sold and was "glad to be rid of." These people who enslaved others, recognized as important people in the settlement of the Cape, had help in all that they did.

Sparse legal records, as well as journals, letters, and books written by captains such as Bangs, Bearse, and Sears, offer a view into the lives of people who were enslaved on the Cape. Elijah Cobb, another captain from Brewster, like so many others, worked the coast, the West Indies, and transatlantic routes. He wrote in his diary—excerpts of which Sears quoted—of a particular instance in 1803 when blockades threatened his return to Europe with a cargo on the ship *William Tell*. Cobb, a good captain and businessman, seemed to take warnings of a shutdown as a challenge—one he clearly decided to overcome by getting out ahead of the blockade.

"About sunrise I went to the 'lazy corner,' so called, and pressed into service every negro that came upon the stand and sent them on board the ship, until I thought there were as many as could work,"[6] Cobb wrote. He succeeded in loading his ship and beating the clock and fulfilling his contract. Did he purchase people to complete the job he'd been hired to do? Was the stand to which he referred an auction block? Were the enslaved people hired out by those who enslaved them, as often happened? It's difficult to tell, because Cobb wrote in his personal journal in language familiar to his time and trade. What became of the people pressed into service? Nothing is said, but Cobb did succeed in delivering his cargo. Several years later, Cobb was aboard the ship *Ten Brothers*. Cobb, along with other men from Brewster, made up the crew on the voyage that left Boston in 1818, thirty-five years after slavery was made illegal in Massachusetts. After spending several months off the West Coast of Africa, many on board contracted yellow fever and died. Cobb sailed the ship back to Boston, stopping in Martinique to unload an "unspecified cargo." Cobb publicly refuted any participation in illegal slave trading, but a darkness hovers at the edges of accounts of the ship and its voyage.

International trafficking of people aside, illicit smuggling was common, and captains and merchants continued to transport humans kidnapped from Africa despite US laws banning the practice. And even though

international importation was banned, the population of people who were enslaved continued to grow as people were born to those who were enslaved. Bearse's description above of Cape Cod's captains legally carrying cargos that included people up and down the southern coast confirms that fortunes continued to be made in domestic trade that included shipments of people being bought and sold by people who were enslavers.

And it wasn't people alone, but also the products they grew, harvested, and created that bolstered fortunes. Captains, including Eben Linnell of Orleans, who began his career aboard the *Buena Vista*, made a good living moving cotton from the South to ports in the North. The relationship between the North and South was what Senator Charles Sumner called an "unholy union . . . between the cotton planters and flesh mongers of Louisiana and Mississippi and the cotton spinners and traffickers of New England—between the lords of the lash and the lords of the loom."[7] The cotton used in the mills of Lowell and other towns throughout the state and region came from people enslaved in the South, marking yet another way in which the

Captain Linnell House in Orleans. Captain Ebenezer "Eben" Linnell broke records for speed traveling the globe. While in later life much of his business occurred in the Pacific Ocean, Linnell's career was launched moving cotton up and down the East Coast. *Photo by Susanna Graham-Pye* people of African descent, enslaved by Americans, were responsible for the success of the nation. Cape Cod's captains participated in this shift from mercantilism to industrialism.

Other than Bournedale, Cape Cod had little in the way of large-scale industrial enterprise. At the time those enslaved in Brewster were alive, mills were smaller, intended for the community for grinding grains and fulling wool. Those who were enslaved would have worked alongside their enslavers—and worshiped with them too. The winter wonderland decorations of the churches and homes along Route 6A today would have been absent (Anglicans decorated churches with greens during this period, but Puritans did not), but Christmas was celebrated with church worship and special foods. In his diary, which is held at the Massachusetts Historical Society, Benjamin Bangs wrote on January 4, 1760, "It was the Negro yearly feast last night." It is very likely that the people enslaved by the Bangs family would have gone to Christmas services with the family. What precisely was the "Negro yearly feast"? It's hard to know if Bangs allowed those he enslaved some sort of celebration after Christmas, or if there were deeper roots to the celebration for those who were enslaved. Perhaps their feast was related to traditions brought from places of origin.

At the First Parish Church of Brewster, members today have been working to develop ways to recognize those parishioners who were enslaved by other members of the church years ago. In church records, listed without surnames are Anna, Hamsheir, Hannah, Jack, two people named James, Jesse, Jolly, Mary, Molly, Mille, Oliver, and Sarah. Church records also note five other nameless people who were enslaved and members of the parish. In addition to identifying both the enslaved and their enslavers, church members have been developing plans for commemoration and reparation. That is today. In 1880, Bearse wrote in his book, "In my past days, the system of slavery was not much discussed. I saw these things as others did, without interference." The interference that has arisen since the days of Bearse's experiences—a Civil War, a northern perception different from a southern perception, echoes of a past that whispers and shapes the present—has colored New Englanders' views. Bearse said, "I wish to see [the realities of slavery] no more,"[8] and he worked to that end by participating in the maritime side of the Underground Railroad. For many years, New Englanders' views of their role in the realities of slavery—what Bearse longed not to see—were obscured. Today, many people in New England and around the nation are trying to clear the view to a more accurate telling of history.

Places for Reflection

BREWSTER

BREWSTER HISTORICAL SOCIETY

739 Lower Road, Brewster
41.761788025719994, -70.08763456111348

The Brewster Historical Society is housed in the home of Captain Elijah Cobb. It has been suggested that Cobb was involved in transporting enslaved people. In 1819, the ship *Ten Brothers* docked in Boston after Cobb captained the vessel to Africa on a trading trip. Cobb was accused and cleared of charges that he knowingly brought yellow fever to Boston. Today, the museum is home to the historical society's collection. The home is an example of Georgian architecture and is a display of the wealth accumulated by those profiting in New England's maritime industries of trafficking people and the goods produced by those who were enslaved.

FIRST PARISH CHURCH

1969 Main Street, Brewster
41.7621390333896, -70.08195654576994

The First Parish is so named for the fact it was the town's first church. Originally a Puritan meetinghouse, the church has been a spiritual home for the people of Brewster for centuries. Among those who were parishioners were a number of people who were enslaved in what was first Harwich and later became its own town, Brewster. Current members of the church have traced their ancestors to the church's founders, learning along the way that among these "forefathers" were some who were enslavers. As was often the tradition, people who were enslaved attended church with their enslavers. The church has been working hard to include the reality of the past in its present.

CHAPTER 6

Falmouth and Mashpee—Fugitives

WHEN YOU GET INTO A TIGHT PLACE, AND EVERYTHING GOES AGAINST YOU TILL IT SEEMS AS IF YOU COULDN'T HOLD ON A MINUTE LONGER, NEVER GIVE UP THEN, FOR THAT'S JUST THE PLACE AND TIME THAT THE TIDE'LL TURN.

—HARRIET BEECHER STOWE

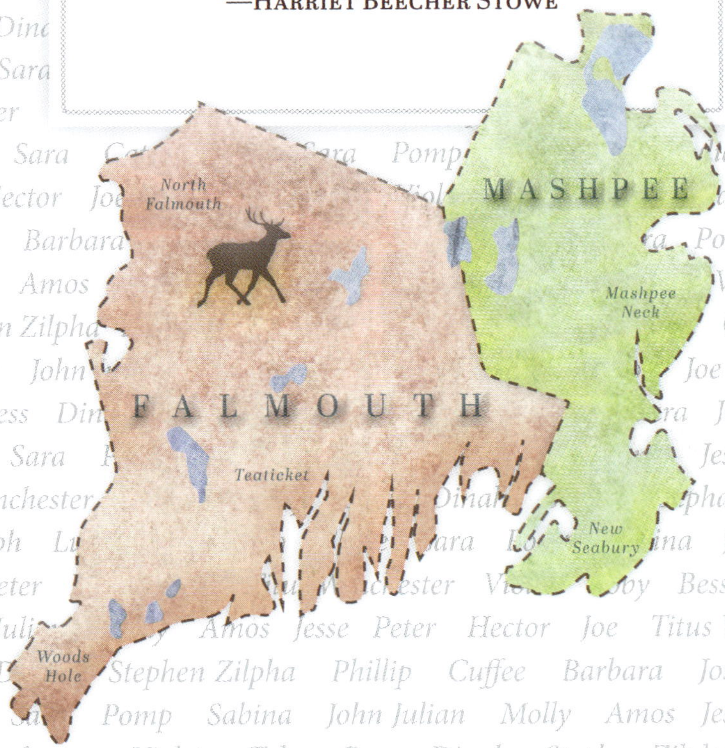

Perfect conditions have to exist to see a pocket sunset over Vineyard Sound out to Buzzards Bay. *Courtesy of* Cape Cod Life

Woods Hole lies at the top of the chain of the Elizabeth Islands in an area where the waters of Buzzards Bay and Vineyard Sound meet. No one is quite sure of the origins of the name Woods Hole, whether it was taken from a surname of someone who once lived along its shores or if it stems from the landscape's appearance: a woody knoll, known as a *holl* in the Norse language of the Vikings, who once sailed these waters. Woods Hole is a name both for the passage of water that connects Great Harbor to Buzzards Bay as well as that of the village. This part of Falmouth, which sits on the shores of Great Harbor, is a wispy tail that trails into the ocean off the elbow of the Cape. The turbulent waters that swirl just offshore are the convergence of four major currents and mirror the push-and-pull influences that have always shaped our history.

On certain August evenings with conditions just right, one can glimpse a perfect "pocket" sunset. Seen only from the south in Vineyard Sound to Buzzards Bay between Falmouth and Naushon Island, it is a rare sight possible only on a few nights at the end of summer evenings. When viewed westward on these special days, the setting sun lines up perfectly between coasts of the land masses of Woods Hole and the Elizabeth Islands as it dips into the waters of Buzzards Bay—a phenomenon that has been likened to a watch being tucked into a gentleman's watch pocket. Unlike the Mayan Seven Dolls Temple, where the sun shines through the structure's aperture one day a year, or Stonehenge's stones built to encircle the sun on solstices, this framing of the sun seen from the vast ocean is nature's doing alone.

Woods Hole, home to the Steamship Authority, links the islands to the mainland and is a place of constant comings and goings. In the summer of 1761, a young man named Peter left Woods Hole. We know about his departure. Of his arrival in Falmouth's village of Woods Hole, however, we know nothing. Did Peter first come to Falmouth by land or sea? From the south? We don't know if, working aboard a packet ship, as some people who were enslaved did, he caught a glimpse of the pocket sunset, that captive sun bound by land. Perhaps having been born on one of the islands of the Caribbean or on a plantation in the South, he would have been traveling north. If he'd come directly from Africa to the docks of Boston where enslaved people were sold, he might have come to Falmouth by land. Arriving from north or south, by land or sea, one way or another Peter came to Falmouth and was enslaved by Ephraim Swift. And Peter, like thousands upon thousands of people, chose to escape his enslavement, leaving Falmouth to find freedom.

On June 28, Peter ran away. His thoughts are not recorded directly, but the sentiments of others living in enslavement are, and they likely reflect his own. Elizabeth Freeman, also known as Mum Bett, of Massachusetts, was purchased in 1742 at the age of six months by John Ashley from Sheffield, Massachusetts. Freeman sued for her freedom and won the case; *Brom and Bett v. Ashley* is often cited as the first legal precedent that ultimately led to the permanent abolition of slavery in Massachusetts. Of her enslavement, Freeman said, "While I was a slave, if one minute's freedom had been offered me, and I had been told I must die at the end of that minute, I would have taken it—just to stand one minute on God's earth, a free woman."[1]

William Wells Brown, a fugitive slave who risked public speaking in support of abolition, wrote about his longing for freedom: "The anxiety to be a freeman would not let me rest day or night. I would think of the northern cities that I had heard so much about—of Canada, where so many of my acquaintances had found refuge. I would dream at night that I was in Canada, a freeman, and on waking in the morning, weep to find myself so sadly mistaken."[2] Brown, who was born fifty-three years after Peter made his escape, lived to see the successes and failures of those who tried to find freedom; he escaped himself and moved to England, where friends ultimately purchased his freedom.

Brown lived to witness the abolition of slavery. Mum Bett was freed and chose a new name for herself: Elizabeth Freeman—her surname a title as much as a name. Peter's quest for freedom took place in a far different landscape. No records were found indicating how long he'd been enslaved by Ephraim Swift. Swift asserted that Peter "spoke good English," which could indicate that English was not his first language. This was not uncommon. Many people kidnapped from the West Coast of Africa spoke a number of European languages, such as Dutch, English, and Portuguese, due to the long-standing presence of trading companies in Africa. Peter would likely have made his escape at night, since, unlike communities in the South with a higher population of people of African descent, New England then, as many communities in this region are still, was predominantly white. A solitary person of color, traveling alone, would draw attention. Also, traveling alone if you were of African or Indian descent was illegal in Massachusetts by this time.

That summer, as Peter left Falmouth, perhaps searching for family, most certainly seeking freedom, the Transit of Venus drew the attention of the world into the sky. Because Venus rarely passes directly in front of the sun, the planet can be viewed on rare occasions as a small black spot moving across the sun at sunrise or sunset. This transit is seen only when Venus travels one of two points and crosses Earth's orbital plane. In Russia that year, scientist Mikhail Lomonosov, one of hundreds watching, observed a ring of light around the planet, leading to the discovery that Venus had an atmosphere. For those who were enslaved that summer, the atmosphere they faced was that of oppression, and Peter was among the hundreds of thousands who attempted to run away during their enslavements. As the watching world recognized the possibility of life on another planet, Peter left Falmouth hoping for a different life as well.

Today, Woods Hole has a global reputation as a center for scientific research. The Woods Hole Oceanographic Institute (WHOI) was founded in 1930 and is a leader in the global study of Earth's oceans. The area was a significant port for mariners long before that. The ocean must have offered a tantalizing suggestion of escape for Peter, whose enslaver's home is now known as the Challenger House on WHOI's campus. Whether Peter's attempt was ultimately successful or not, he left on June 28 with what might be viewed as hope, wearing "a Beaveret Hat, a green worsted Capt, a close bodied Coat colored with a green narrow Frieze Cape, a Great Coat, a black and white homespun Jacket, a flannel checked Shirt, grey yarn Stockings; also a flannel Jacket." Peter carried a bundle of other clothes and a violin. In the advertisement that Swift placed in the *Boston Gazette and Journal*,

The Swift House postcard shows the home from which Peter, a person who was enslaved by Ephraim Swift, ran away. *Courtesy of the Falmouth Historical Society*

he warned readers against any attempts to help Peter, "a very tall fellow," with a promise to prosecute to the fullest those who might try. Swift also offered a five-pound reward for Peter's return.

Peter lived in Massachusetts one hundred years after the first people of African descent were trafficked to the colony aboard the ship *Desire*. His escape attempt in 1761 took place one hundred years before ratification of the Thirteenth Amendment, which stated, "Neither slavery nor involuntary servitude, except as a punishment for crime where of the party shall have been duly convicted, shall exist within the United States, or any place subject to their jurisdiction." But Peter's here and now, the period during which he or perhaps his parents were kidnapped from their birthplace and trafficked into slavery, was moored firmly in the height of the slave trade in New England.

From the time of Massachusetts's leaders' first steps to legalize slavery in the Body of Liberties, laws there and elsewhere in New England were crafted and amended to define and defend the enslavement of people.

This image shows a woman named Ellen Craft, who disguised herself as a white man and, along with her husband, William, escaped enslavement in South Carolina in the mid-1800s. The couple moved to London. The image accompanied an article about them in the *Illustrated London News*.

Enslavement was first protected under the law in Massachusetts Bay Colony in 1641. The passage read: "There shall never be any bond slavery, villinage or captivity amongst us unless it be lawful Captives taken in just wars, and such strangers as willingly sell themselves or are sold to us." In 1670, Massachusetts's General Court removed the word "stranger." Strangers, at that point in time, could be defined as those who were different, people indigenous to the Americas, or African. Simply removing the word "stranger" made slavery permanent and hereditary.

Cape Cod and Massachusetts—in fact all of New England—were part of a larger, global web. The Puritans and others from England and parts of Europe who settled in colonies had left behind homes in nations where the institution of slavery had long been present in their daily lives. Fugitive slave laws emerged hand in hand with the practice of enslavement. Before colonization in North American, laws about the return of fugitives were established in West African nations and among Europe's peoples, including the Spanish, Portuguese, and Dutch. Among the first formal so-called fugitive slave laws in the North American colonies was a clause in the Articles of Confederation of the New England Confederation of Plymouth, Massachusetts, Connecticut, and New Haven: "If any servant run away from his master into any of these Confederated Jurisdictions, that in such case, upon the certificate of one magistrate in the jurisdiction out of which the servant had fled or upon other due proof, the said servant shall be delivered either to his master or to any other that pursues and brings such certificate or proof." Little about the law changed. In almost identical forms, the clause made it into bodies of law in 1787, 1793, and 1850.

At least half the delegates who attended the Constitutional Convention in Philadelphia enslaved people or had been enslavers, and the issue of slavery was a central debate in the proceedings. The authors of the Constitution ultimately intentionally left the issue of slavery out of the document, knowing that any kind of restriction on the institution would stall the Constitution's approval. Debates over federal regulation of slavery and a deep belief that states should independently have control over the issue threatened to divide the country and evoked threats from the South of leaving the newborn nation. While the words "slave" and "slavery" are not in the Constitution, the three-fifths law that determined states' representation and taxation based on population—"excluding Indians not taxed, three fifths of all other Persons"—formalized the belief that people who were enslaved did not count as fully human.

In 1793, the first federal Fugitive Slave Act was enacted. The law gave federal and circuit judges as well as states the ability to rule on the fate of enslaved people who had escaped their enslavers. It protected those who returned people to their enslavers and punished those who helped people reach freedom. Some historians argue that the law helped with the creation of the Underground Railroad. Slavery had been abolished in Massachusetts at this point for ten years, but people who helped those fleeing were still subject to legal punishment. By 1850, when the second Fugitive Slave Act became law, the nation was mired in an increasingly complex debate over its growth, its economy, and the role of human trafficking in all of it. This new federal act made laws across the states more uniform, taking away people's right to a jury, inflicting extreme fines on those who assisted people who were escaping enslavement, and making it legally required that all people who'd escaped be returned to enslavement, even if they were found in free states.

Like so much of the narrative that includes this country's role in the story of human trafficking, the chapter on the Underground Railroad is told in a black/white, North/South way: people enslaved in the South escaped to go north. For thousands, this was made possible with the help of people working illegally (underground) in a coordinated network (the railroad) moving enslaved people north. If the areas to which they fled were "free states," laws there still protected their enslavers and punished those who helped people who were enslaved. The Underground Railroad most familiar to the general public today was the one operating at its height during the early to mid-nineteenth century. Cape Cod, its Quakers, and some of its laypeople, ship captains, and merchants helped form the network as much as Cape Codders helped create the need for it. What assistance was available to Peter, though, in 1761? Did he follow the North Star? Probably not, since Peter's north was one in which enslavement was legal and active. Canada, a destination for many who traveled the Underground Railroad, did not abolish slavery until 1834, when the British Parliament passed the Slavery Abolition Act, abolishing slavery in most of its empire. Where did Peter want to go? Probably east, maybe south; whichever direction, it was most certainly in search of home, family, and love.

While it appears that an organized system to help people escape enslavement didn't begin until the end of the eighteenth century, the Quakers may have started a network earlier. George Washington wrote that a "society of Quakers, formed for such purposes," attempted to assist the escape of one of the people he enslaved.[3] Cape Cod, particularly the upper Cape and the islands to which Falmouth has always been closely connected, was home to many Quakers. The first Quakers arrived on Cape Cod in the middle of the seventeenth century. Unlike Massachusetts Bay Colony, where being a Quaker could mean execution, Plymouth Colony persecuted the Quakers mostly with heavy fines, though some people who were Quakers there were punished with enslavement. One reason for the Quakers' success on this slim peninsula was settlers who tended toward an Anabaptist philosophy that predated the expansion of other denominations and supported the separation of church and state, more inclusive practices, and pacifism. One of those was Edward Freeman of Sandwich. The Quakers of Cape Cod and the islands also dominated the whaling industry, another unique aspect of life on the Cape, and many of the crews aboard ships sailing for Quaker companies consisted of people of African descent who lived as free men.

Did Peter find freedom aboard a whaling ship? Perhaps he did; there is no mention of him in Ephraim Swift's will. Maybe Peter sailed the oceans of the world as a free person, traveling around the Cape of Good Hope, spending years at sea, and seeing different countries and cultures—seeing more of the world than his enslavers ever would. It's possible, but most people who

A New England whaler. *Courtesy of US Library of Congress*

tried to escape were caught. A handful, though, succeeded. We can hope that this was Peter's fate, and that he could experience what William Wells Brown, who successfully escaped his enslavement, described: "The fact that I was in all probability a freeman sounded in my ears like a charm. I am satisfied that none but a slave could place such an appreciation upon liberty as I did at that time. I wanted to see mother and sister, that I might tell them 'I was free!'"[4]

Places for Reflection

FALMOUTH AND MASHPEE

WOODS HOLE STEAMSHIP PIERS

1 Cowdry Road, Falmouth
41.761788025719994, -70.08763456111348

The Steamship Authority was created by the Massachusetts legislature in 1960, establishing transportation between Barnstable Harbor and Woods Hole and the islands of Martha's Vineyard and Nantucket. The piers are a wonderful place to watch the comings and goings between the mainland and the islands—and to imagine those who arrived. A trip to the Vineyard offers visitors a tour of the Martha's Vineyard African American Heritage Trail. Also, the Museum of African American History in Boston has a Nantucket campus, comprising two buildings: the African Meeting House and the Florence Higginbotham House, buildings important to the community on Nantucket, particularly for residents of African descent.

WOOD HOLE OCEANOGRAPHIC INSTITUTE (WHOI)

86 Water Street, Falmouth
41.524685123965796, -70.66837402912243

What is today the Challenger House on the campus of the Woods Hole Oceanographic Institute was once called home by Ephraim Swift, who enslaved a young man named Peter. The building was Peter's home too until he escaped in the summer of 1761. Swift ran an ad in a Boston newspaper offering a reward for Peter's return. Whether Peter succeeded in his attempt to find freedom is unclear.

CHAPTER 7

Chatham and Harwich – Churches

> *WERE IT NOT FOR PERSONS IN HIGH PLACES OWNING SLAVES, AND THEREBY GIVING THE SYSTEM A REPUTATION, AND ESPECIALLY PROFESSED CHRISTIANS, SLAVERY WOULD LONG SINCE HAVE BEEN ABOLISHED.*
>
> —W. W. BROWN,
> *Clotel, or The President's Daughter*

The First Congregational Church in Harwich could have been one of the churches from which parishioners left to attend the Abolition Rally on that fourth day of the multiday rally in August 1848. Many of the people attending participated in an angry riot that newspapers of the day called "the Harwich Mob." *Photo by Susanna Graham-Pye*

Wind moves through the grove's old cedar-scented pine boughs sounding like water. The air has traveled over the ocean, picking up hints of salty, colder depths, bringing them inland, pushing through the branches making rivers of sound. Leaves flip and roll in the currents, revealing minnow-silver underbellies, a sign seen by most in these maritime parts as an indication a thunderstorm could be on its way. The dance between land and sea breezes on hot days near the shore creates a summer blessing strong enough to move heavy humid salt air, and in Harwich, on Sunday, the last day of August 1848, people needed such a blessing. Temperatures during that long-ago summer had been record breaking, and, unfortunately, the rains didn't fall as the late-day storms popped up alongside the prevailing southwest winds, as they often did. The clouds instead skirted north, avoiding the beckoning arm of the Cape.

An antislavery rally being held in what was called the Grove had gone well to this point. The multiday event had been planned by the Massachusetts Anti-Slavery Society, the organization that had grown out of the New England Anti-Slavery Society created by William Lloyd Garrison a decade earlier. The group sponsored "agents," or speakers, to travel throughout the region advocating for the abolition of slavery. The most significant speakers attending the Harwich event were William Wells Brown, Parker Pillsbury, Stephen Symonds Foster, and Lucy Stone.

For three days, events had been relatively calm. The convention was organized by Harwich's Captain Zebina Small and other abolitionists on the Cape. Small, as many men of the sea did, would go on to work in the cranberry industry. An avid abolitionist, Small often hosted antislavery speakers who spoke at rallies around the country. On this day, a perfect emotional storm was brewing as a speaker who was currently a fugitive slave and a woman speaker stood on stage alongside two men who questioned the veracity of the church's stance and teaching. And then there was the heat. It was as though tempers had been tethered to the thermometer's mercury, which had risen over the course of the convention to more and more oppressive heights.

William Wells Brown must have caused a ripple of anxiety as he stepped forward, because—whether those in attendance approved of it or not—the law said slaves were to be returned even if they were in a "free state." The hot wind cooled him only slightly. Brown was a popular speaker on the

Image of William Wells Brown. Brown spoke at the rally in Harwich in 1848 and was attacked by antiabolitionists. Brown was an abolitionist, women's-rights activist, speaker, playwright, novelist, and travel writer. After escaping from his enslaver, Brown traveled to the northern states as a speaker. He ultimately moved to London, England, where friends paid for his freedom.

abolitionists' circuit. He had been known to hold audiences' attention for hours. He wiped his forehead as he stood on the platform staring out over the Harwich Mob—which is what the newspapers and history would come to call the gathering of people on this day. And, as anger always is, it was an ugly sight, the kind that Brown often tried to describe in his depiction of the experiences of those living in slavery.

Brown often said he would "fail to represent the real condition of the slave [because] slavery can never be represented." But even though he could never evoke true empathy, he would continue to try to at least generate sympathy to help the cause of freeing people living in enslavement. In his autobiography, *From Fugitive Slave to Free Man*, Brown said this of waiting for the opportunity to escape:

> During the last night that I served in slavery, I did not close my eyes a single moment. When not thinking of the future, my mind dwelt on the past. The love of a dear mother, a dear sister, and three dear brothers, yet living, caused me to shed many tears. If I could only have been assured of their being dead, I should have felt satisfied; but I imagined I saw my dear mother in the cotton field, followed by a merciless task-master, and no one to speak a consoling word to her! I beheld my dear sister in the hands of a slave-driver, and compelled to submit to his cruelty! None but one placed in such a situation can for a moment imagine the intense agony to which these reflections subjected me.[1]

Brown's lectures were called "riveting" and "soul stirring." However, not everyone in the audience in Harwich on this particular Sunday was sympathetic.

Brown was the first American of African descent who had been enslaved to publish a novel. He was a playwright and a travel writer. Brown was born in Kentucky while his mother was enslaved there. His father was the man who enslaved her. After a number of failed attempts to escape, Brown succeeded. He described how he had planned for his escape when the captain for whom he worked, a man by the name of Price, decided to take a boat on which Brown was a steward, from New Orleans to Ohio:

> Captain Price had some fears as to the propriety of taking me near a free State or a place where it was likely I could run away with a prospect of liberty. He asked me if I had ever been in a free State. "Oh yes," said I, "I have been in Ohio; my master carried me into that State once, but I never liked a free State." It was soon decided that it would be safe to take me with them, and what made

> it more safe, Eliza was on the boat with us, and Mrs. Price, to try me, asked if I thought as much as ever of Eliza. I told her that Eliza was very dear to me indeed, and that nothing but death should part us. It was the same as if we were married. This had the desired effect. The boat left New Orleans, and proceeded up the river.

While this personal narrative describes his life and escape, Brown's novel *Clotel* explores the duality of Christianity in the institution of slavery both as a tool of oppression used by people who enslaved other people and as a source of hope and community for people living in enslavement. At the time of the Harwich Rally and the angry reaction it evoked among many people in the area, the Great Awakening (sometimes called the Second Awakening) was in full swing. The awakening was one wave in a larger set sweeping across the country and, in some cases, the world. Temperance, women's rights, and abolition were also among the reforms being demanded by increasing numbers of people. The period was a notable one during which the cultural and racial caste systems constructed by a wealthy white elite class were being questioned. Brown and the other speakers present that day were active in all these fights.

As the nation matured, it seemed as if the population had entered a kind of adolescence, a period when the rigid positions of forefathers were being rejected. In its earliest colonial days, the concept of slavery was defended vehemently from the pulpit by the religious leaders of the times. In one of his sermons, Cotton Mather told parishioners who "have any NEGROES in your Houses" that they had an

> Opportunity to try, Whether you may not be the Happy Instruments, of Converting, the Blackest Instances of Blindness and Baseness, into admirable Candidates of Eternal Blessedness. Let not this Opportunity be Lost; if you have any concern for Souls, your Own or Others; but, make a Trial, Whether by your Means, the most Brutish of Creatures upon Earth may not come to be disposed, in some Degree, like the Angels of Heaven; and the Vassals of Satan, become the Children of God. . . . It is come to pass by the Providence of God, without which there comes nothing to pass, that Poor NEGROES are cast under your Government and Protection. . . . Who can tell but that this Poor Creature may belong to the Election of God! Who can tell, but that God may have sent this Poor Creature into my Hands, that so One of the Elect may by my means be Called; & by my Instruction be made Wise unto Salvation! The glorious God will put an unspeakable Glory upon me, if it may be so![2]

In the eighteenth century, many of the Cape's religious leaders—men such as Reverend Lord of Chatham and Edmund Freeman of Sandwich, as well as deacons such as Shubael Taylor in Yarmouth and John Freeman in Eastham—enslaved people. Reverend Abraham Williams, who became the pastor of Sandwich's First Parish Church in 1749, enslaved a man named Titus Winchester. Williams, upon his death, freed Winchester in his will. Winchester, who went to sea, died in 1808 and left his estate to the First Parish, specifying that the money be used to buy a clock for the church tower. While the telling of this story recounts Winchester's gift as a token of his love for Williams, a clock in a steeple could symbolize the time stolen from people, the time it has taken for people to begin the hard process of reconciling reality with romantic recollections, and the time it will take to undo the damages of the past.

Clearly, the role of Christianity in supporting the practice of enslavement was as troublesome as the country's foundational principles of equality and liberty were in the face of slavery. In the uncertainty that began alongside crafting state constitutions across the new nation, documents in which "all men" were being declared equal, the issue of enslavement was threatening to tear the country apart. The religious ideals preached by those such as Mather and the economic arguments made by the earliest colonists that slavery was critical to building the nation were increasingly in conflict with ideals argued by the four speakers who had stopped in Harwich as they traveled the New England region.

Much of the property at Bells Neck is thought to have been purchased by John Bell in 1668, from people native to the area called Saquatucket. Today, the preserve offers walking paths, peaceful places for reflection, and stellar birdwatching. It also protects the Herring River, West Reservoir. *Photo by Susanna Graham-Pye*

Lucy Stone had graduated from college the previous spring and just been hired by the Massachusetts Anti-Slavery Society. She was the only woman to speak at the rally. Despite her mother's concerns for her safety and liberal Oberlin College's refusal to let her train as a public speaker, Lucy had persevered and was living the life she wanted. Her fight for an education had been a long one. She was twenty-nine when she graduated and had just turned thirty when she began working for the society. Despite facing resistance from every corner of her world, Lucy was determined to be a public speaker for "not the slave only, but for suffering humanity everywhere."

Lucy explained to her mother that she understood the perils facing her in her chosen vocation to speak and fight for suffering, oppressed people:

> Mother, I know you too well to suppose that you would wish me to turn away from what I think is my duty. . . . I surely would not be a public speaker if I sought a life of ease, for it will be a most laborious one. Nor would I do it for the sake of honor, for I know I will be disesteemed, nay even hated by some who are now friends or profess to be.[3]

Parker Pillsbury, who frequently appeared with Lucy, had grown up on a New Hampshire farm. He was a gentle person who shunned violence in all forms, though he was often the recipient of it during lecture events such as this one.

As the convention hours and days passed, reasons for agitation among the crowd collected into angry pockets. Lucy's appearance on the speaking platform was unsettling to the audiences simply for the unfamiliarity of a woman speaking so strongly. Pillsbury's words often, if not always, caused agitation for his calling out the church practices he believed endorsed and perpetuated people's enslavement. Pillsbury had already been stripped of his license to preach as a Methodist minister because of his criticisms of the church. Despite opposition to his stance from many, even some fighting the same battle, Pillsbury bravely adhered to his beliefs, describing a Christianity that was based on "complexional salvation." He said,

> The Methodist Discipline provides for "separate Colored Conferences." The Episcopal church shuts out some of its own most worthy ministers from clerical recognition, on account of their color. Nearly all denominations of religionists have either a written or unwritten law to the same effect. In Boston, even, there are Evangelical churches whose pews are positively forbidden by corporate mandate from being sold to any but "respectable white persons." Our incorporated cemeteries are often, if not always, deeded

in the same manner. Even our humblest village grave yards generally have either a "negro corner," or refuse colored corpses altogether; and did our power extend to heaven or hell, we should have complexional salvation and colored damnation.[4]

Even though violence often greeted them at engagements where they spoke, Pillsbury was known for responding to hostility and violence with nonviolence.

Whereas Parker was a pacifist, Stephen Symonds Foster was known to be aggressive and intense, often provoking incidents among the audiences to which he spoke. His anger was stoked by his belief that the people filling church pews—people claiming to be Christians—had a duty to speak out against slavery. He often attended churches in the towns where he was lecturing, quietly taking his place among parishioners, only to rise at some point during the service and condemn the institution, calling it the very "bulwark" of slavery.

The fourth and final day of the Harwich Rally was different. It was, after all, Sunday, the day of worship, and a local captain, Stillman Snow, having heard of Foster's comments and having just been to church, arrived in the grove shouting that what Foster said was "a damned lie."

Summer clouds, often of fair-weather ilk, can quickly gather into thunderheads and move across the land. *Photos by Susanna Graham-Pye*

The onshore breeze wandered through the crowd, lifting the bunting that hung across the bottom of the platform and pushing onward, taking with it rustling bits of leaflets dropped after they'd been read.

Another angry captain arrived after hearing that Foster had told the story of "a captain of the area" who'd been asked by a "fugitive slave" in Norfolk, Virginia, for help escaping to the North. The captain had taken $100 from the person, only to return him and the money to his enslaver. The captain earned a $25 reward for his efforts. Foster said that the captain, who was known to be a devout, churchgoing man, was further proof of the church's depravity.

On this fourth day of the rally, Brown spoke of his own experiences as well as the larger concerns of the time, including slavery and abolition. He asked his audience to consider how Christianity and slavery could possibly coexist. Not everyone in the audience in Harwich on this particular Sunday was sympathetic.

"Tar and feather him," someone yelled.

"Ride him out on a rail," another voice rose.

"Pass out that nigger," said yet another angry shout.[5]

Unlike the passing thunderstorms that hadn't reached Harwich, this emotional storm broke out in a mob estimated to be anywhere between one thousand and three thousand people strong.

"Havoc was soon made of our platform and what it contained," according to Parker. The raised temporary structure had a roof over it to protect the speakers, officers of the meeting, and older residents. It was destroyed.

"William Wells Brown, one of our eloquent fugitive slave lecturers, was roughly seized up and pitched over back of the platform by the infuriated crowd down some six or eight feet, and left to his fate," Parker continued. And his friend Foster "was rescued and taken away from danger—his Sunday frock coat rent in twain from bottom to top, and his body considerably battered and bruised."[6]

Underscoring his belief that nonviolence was the only response to violence, Parker said he believed it was Lucy's "serene, quiet bearing [that] disarmed the vulgar villainy of our assailants."[7] She was not hurt.

The incident, widely reported in local and regional papers of the time, highlights the role of the North in the chattel slave trade. Massachusetts was the first colony to make slavery legal. Cape Cod's seaports were the nursery for the dozens of sea captains who participated in the trade and enslavement of humans. And, until the early 1800s, many Cape families enslaved people.

"I have seen many mobs and riots in my more than 40 years of humble service in the cause of freedom and humanity, but I never encountered one more desperate in determination, nor fiendish in spirit, than was that in Harwich in the year 1848," Parker concluded.[8]

Places for Reflection

CHATHAM AND HARWICH

PLEASANT BAY WOODLANDS

75 Kendrick Road, Harwich
41.71766029375818, −70.00547856901609

The Pleasant Bay Woodlands were purchased by the Harwich Conservation Trust. Walking trails lead people past a cranberry bog and around open field space that is being replanted with indigenous Cape Cod plants. The property was purchased in a transaction between the Kendrick family and the Indigenous people of the region in the 1700s. Edward Kendrick bequeathed as many as six people to his wife and children. Those people who were enslaved very well might have lived on the property and certainly worked on it, farming, herding, and harvesting.

MUDDY CREEK HEADWATERS PRESERVE

In Harwich off Church Street
41.697454380325524, -69.99382054271487
(Coordinates shown are for the river itself.)

Muddy Creek Preserve is protected by Harwich Conservation Trust. This land along the banks of the Muddy River is known to be sacred among the Indigenous people of the area. It was a feasting site where the leaders of Wampanoag communities gathered, and it is thought to be the land on which Tisquantum helped William Bradford negotiate with the people who were native to the area for food. It looks out over Pleasant Bay toward the ocean, over the land where Tisquantum is thought to have been buried.

CHAPTER 8

Orleans—Connections

HISTORY WANTS US TO BELIEVE THAT THE INDIAN WAS A SAVAGE, ILLITERATE, UNCIVILIZED ANIMAL. A HISTORY THAT WAS WRITTEN BY AN ORGANIZED, DISCIPLINED PEOPLE, TO EXPOSE US AS AN UNORGANIZED AND UNDISCIPLINED ENTITY. TWO DISTINCTLY DIFFERENT CULTURES MET. ONE THOUGHT THEY MUST CONTROL LIFE; THE OTHER BELIEVED LIFE WAS TO BE ENJOYED, BECAUSE NATURE DECREED IT. LET US REMEMBER, THE INDIAN IS AND WAS JUST AS HUMAN AS THE WHITE MAN. THE INDIAN FEELS PAIN, GETS HURT, AND BECOMES DEFENSIVE, HAS DREAMS, BEARS TRAGEDY AND FAILURE, SUFFERS FROM LONELINESS, NEEDS TO CRY AS WELL AS LAUGH. HE, TOO, IS OFTEN MISUNDERSTOOD.

—WAMSUTTA (FRANK B.) JAMES,
from the suppressed speech that was to be given at the 350th Thanksgiving Celebration in Plymouth, Massachusetts, in 1970

Sunrise over Pleasant Bay. *Photo by Susanna Graham-Pye*

The sun moves steadily from the other side of the world but is still beneath the horizon. Close enough to the edge to brighten the sky—deep indigo to opal orange and blue. Not a whisper of wind ruffles the mirror surface of the water, beneath which a massive school of pogies move like one long river. Their sequin silver scales tip the colors of sky and clouds and water, making them something marvelous, something otherworldly, but it's not another world. It's this world. Their world. Our world.

The fish break the stillness, sending noise and froth into the air, boiling the surface as the pack of bluefish that has been stalking them strikes. The wakening breeze fills with the oily brine scent of the blues. Out where the water is still smooth, in unbroken reflection, is the rounded head of a seal who watches, waiting for the fish to head his way. The drops of moisture in the hazy summer sky catch the light of the sun as it breaks over the edge of the earth, making the air glisten with the promise of a beautiful day.

A mysterious, indefinable presence fills the Pleasant Bay estuary. The very best of nature's bounty can be found here. The barrier beach, a classic element of these kinds of systems, lies between the marsh, with its winding channels, and the mighty Atlantic. The shifting dunes, slowly rolling landward, are home to a migrating breach made by winter storms. The breakthrough replenishes the bay with fresh ocean waters and a wide fluctuation of tides. The breach always moves in a northerly direction, and when it has passed, the bay settles, bars grow and stabilize until the arrival of some new winter storm, and the breach returns south to begin its northerly trek again.

The islands of the bay—Hog Island, Sipson's Island, Little Sipson, Strong Island, and Pochet—crouch behind the marsh. Hog Island is rumored to be one of the places the pirate Captain Kidd buried treasure. Legends say Kidd buried treasure in many places throughout coastal New England, and Hog Island in the Gloucester area also lays claim to unfound loot. The tale tells of Kidd—trying to escape capture, scooting out of the Atlantic into Pleasant Bay—burying what treasure he carried, then proceeding to take a shortcut through Jeremiah's Gutter into Cape Cod Bay. The shores of Pleasant Bay, legend holds, are where Tisquantum, more popularly known as Squanto, was buried in 1622 off the point of land, now located in the town today called Chatham. In all likelihood, the land is no longer there after years of erosion, and Tisquantum, the native of Patuxet, is long gone into the sea. A plaque on a boulder claiming to mark his burial place has resided in several different places in town.

The people who are indigenous to Cape Cod have always understood the sacred nature of the Pleasant Bay estuary system. Connecting the ocean and bay to inland ponds, Muddy Creek was called Askaonkton, "at the Wading Place." A sign on Route 28 just before the bridge over the creek points out that being "at" a place and being "on" Cape Cod are a vernacular that denotes a sense of "place memory," a sense that is disappearing. People, however, are trying to hold on to that sense of place and, in many cases, restore truth to the memories made there. An appropriate visual for those efforts is the creek itself. For nearly a hundred years, the culvert allowing the Muddy Creek to run beneath Route 28 strangled the waterway, nearly killing the system of marshes and the anadromous fish run it fed. However, the culvert, which had been installed when Route 28 was constructed, was removed, restoring the natural tidal flow, and the river and surrounding ecosystems are recovering.

Long before Route 28, paved roads, and even dirt pathways, the people who lived there relatively undisturbed for thousands of years used the river as a boundary between seasons. In the fall, men and women gathered along its shores. They buried the canoes deep in the mud for the winter season. The boats, some 40 or 50 feet long, were carved from hickory, elm, and ash trees that filled the old-growth forests surrounding the bay. Some of the trees could have been 30 feet around, and the boats resembled those of Pacific Islanders. Burying boats in the river protected the crafts from the threat of drying out and cracking. The people harvested shellfish and marsh reeds and grass to be woven into mats for winter dwellings.

In the spring, the river, like many on the Cape, connected ocean and inland ponds. People returned to the river's shores, dug up the boats, and harvested the migrating anadromous fish: herring, shad, and salmon. Eels could also be found in the brackish water. Archeological evidence suggests that the banks of Muddy Creek hosted important ceremonial feasting places for the people who were native to the area. It is thought by some to be where Tisquantum, who was among the first people to be captured and trafficked from this region, came with William Bradford to negotiate for corn seed in 1622.

The Harwich Conservation Trust Muddy Creek Headwaters Preserve protects 17 acres of open space on the Muddy River. Walking trails wander through forests that are sacred to the Indigenous people of this area, and offer spectacular views of the river. *Courtesy of Stephanie Foster*

Tisquantum was born in Patuxet, the area where the Pilgrims chose to settle and called Plymouth. One among fifteen men kidnapped and trafficked to Spain to be sold as slaves, his story is heartbreaking, as much for his enslavement as for his escape from it. Tisquantum made it back, to home and freedom, only to find that his entire family had perished in what is known as "the Great Dying." The identity of the disease that killed so many

The loom pictured here is very much like what would have been used by any of the people of European descent living on Cape Cod during the eighteenth century. This loom, found at the Nye Homestead and Museum in Sandwich, is thought to have been built around the time of the American Revolution. *Photo by Susanna Graham-Pye*

Native populations in the Northeast is still a topic of research and debate. Smallpox, yellow fever, influenza, chicken pox, typhoid fever, meningitis, and other diseases have been suspected over the years.[1] Thomas Hunt, who kidnapped the people from Patuxet, failed to sell the men as he hoped in Spain. As a result, Tisquantum wound up in London, England, in the home of John Slaney. Through Slaney, who was the treasurer of the Newfoundland Company, Tisquantum traveled to Newfoundland as a guide. There, he met Thomas Dermer, an adventurer, whom Tisquantum convinced to bring him home. After five years away, Tisquantum arrived to find nearly all in his community dead. Having lived among people in England for five years, Tisquantum spoke English fluently and found a role translating for the colonists. In 1622, after accompanying Bradford to Pleasant Bay to help negotiate food for the coming winter, Tisquantum died. He was not the only person who was enslaved to walk the shores of Pleasant Bay.

Some ninety years after Tisquantum's death, Edward Kendrick arrived in what is today South Orleans. With no explanations of why or elaboration as to how, Kendrick is often described as "very close to Cape Cod Indians."[2] Kendrick came to the area to buy land, and much of what he acquired was in the Pleasant Bay system. He had property between Arey's and Portanimicut Ponds, from there stretching across the peninsula to the Cape Cod Bay side of Orleans around Baker's Pond. He purchased much of it from John Sipson, a person who was native to the area. One deed conveying property from Sipson to Kendrick mentions Sipson's love for Kendrick, underscoring Kendrick's positive relations with the people who were native to this part of Cape Cod. While the area in and around Pleasant Bay was Kendrick's first purchase, he also acquired land around Muddy Creek and Round Cove. He owned 15 acres in Truro as well at the time of his death.

Kendrick was a weaver and merchant. He had livestock and extensive grazing land, fields for planting, and woodlots. He built a large home. For all of this, Kendrick used the labor of the people of African descent whom he enslaved. In addition to being a weaver, Kendrick was known as a "dealer," which meant he was a store owner or merchant. In colonial times, the general store of any area met many critical needs. Kendrick would have sold items such as coffee, tea, and sugar as well as barrels, tools, and metal goods. Cheese, clothing, candles, furs—whatever settlers needed, Kendrick would have found, harvested, hunted, or made.

The people who were enslaved by Kendrick would have helped to make, hunt, or harvest much of what was sold. And whether he was such good friends with the Indigenous people called Indians because he'd purchased so much land or if they sold him so much land because they

Sheep grazing in marshes and pastures across Cape Cod were a common sight. Wool was essential for clothing, and most towns had their own fulling mills. *Photo by Susanna Graham-Pye*

A view over the marsh toward Pochet Island. Site of, according to some deeds, "negroes homes" and where the *Mary Anne* wrecked the night the *Whydah Gally* went down off Wellfleet. Some records say the crew of the *Mary Anne* intentionally beached the vessel. *Photo by Susanna Graham-Pye*

were such good friends is a chicken-or-egg kind of mystery. No matter, Kendrick and his family and the people he enslaved lived in an area along-side many people whose ancestors had been here for hundreds, if not thousands, of years.

Off Kendrick Road in Harwich, the Harwich Conservation Trust (HCT) owns another parcel called Pleasant Bay Woodlands. This land was Kendrick's and could have included the site of his original homestead. Today, the HCT is restoring a large part of the property to native meadowland. Deer and owls are frequent visitors at dawn and dusk. In Harwich, near the cranberry bog that abuts the preserve, there is a large stand of white cedar trees, a rare sight today but common enough during colonial times. Prized for their strength,

the trees were tended by the people indigenous to the area, who rarely cut them down. They harvested the trees' bark for various uses. When Sipson spoke of his love for Kendrick being a reason he sold the property to Kendrick, he also cited the negotiated retention of certain land use rights. This stand of fragrant, hearty trees may have been the one mentioned in one of the deeds of sale to Kendrick. Although Kendrick owned the land, the people who were native to the area retained rights to the cedar trees.

How many people Kendrick enslaved over his years here, and for how long, doesn't seem to be mentioned in what is written about him. However, at the time of his death, Kendrick enslaved seven people. None of these people are given ages in his will, but their names are listed. There was

Phillip, left to Kendrick's son, Solomon, and Zilpha, bequeathed to his daughter, Susannah. Four people, Cuffee, Barbara, Joseph, and Luce, were to remain with Kendrick's wife, Deborah. Kendrick passed away around 1742, several decades before slavery was abolished in Massachusetts. Whether or not the people enslaved by his family—Phillip, Zilpha, Cuffee, Barbara, Joseph, and Luce—were alive at the time their freedom became a right under Massachusetts law is a mystery. We do know that Solomon emigrated from the Cape to Nova Scotia; perhaps he took Phillip. If so, was Phillip taken from a family he loved?

Somewhere near Kendrick's home in South Orleans was a Native burial ground used by Indigenous people of the area. The mounds of those graves were evident into the nineteenth century. Perhaps this was a place that might accept those the Kendricks enslaved, or perhaps they were buried on the shores of the lands the family owned in Pleasant Bay. Wherever they were buried, Phillip, Zilpha, Cuffee, Susannah, Barbara, and Joseph spent their lives on the lands that crouch behind the Nauset Beach's dunes. The tides, sunrises and sunsets, migrations, and weather of the bay would have dictated their days as much as the Kendricks did.

Night falls as beautifully as days dawn here. Sometimes, in a rare spectacle, the gentle waves pushed inward by the full moon are filled with bioluminescence, turning the shifting currents into a luminous blue green. A hand drawn through the water of the bay on such nights can illuminate a magical trail over which gentle breezes whisper out of the darkness with voices from the past.

Places for Reflection

ORLEANS

CAPTAIN LINNELL HOUSE

137 Skaket Beach Road, Orleans
41.79863940018432, -70.01189182473396

The Captain Linnell house, a neoclassic villa, was designed and built after the Linnells visited France. The design was drawn from the home of one of Linnell's French business associates. For decades, the grand structure housed a fine restaurant and was a popular site for wedding receptions. It has since returned to private ownership and is no longer open to the public. There is no evidence that Linnell enslaved people; however, he began to accumulate his ultimately substantial wealth from his prosperous maritime business shipping cotton from southern plantations to northern factories.

PLEASANT BAY—SIPSON'S ISLAND

41.73821798349717, -69.96339216989048

Pleasant Bay is a state-designated Area of Critical Environmental Concern. The estuary sits behind a barrier system of marsh and beach. Sipson's Island at the head of the bay—sold in 1711 by Native people to people settling the area—has recently been acquired and is now protected by a land trust. While it is open to the public, access is challenging. No commercial boats are allowed, and single-town landings provide limited access and parking for launching. The trust's work includes restoring the island to its undeveloped, natural state. The island offers a beautiful vantage of the bay, the barrier beach, and the world that shaped the lives of those who lived here during colonial days.

CHAPTER 9

Wellfleet—Ships and Whales

“ALL READY?” CRIED THE CAPTAIN;
“AY, AY!” THE SEAMEN SAID;
“HEAVE UP THE WORTHLESS LUBBERS,—
THE DYING AND THE DEAD.”
UP FROM THE SLAVE-SHIP’S PRISON
FIERCE, BEARDED HEADS WERE THRUST
“NOW LET THE SHARKS LOOK TO IT,—
TOSS UP THE DEAD ONES FIRST!”

—JOHN GREENLEAF WHITTER

White-tail deer continue to be plentiful on Cape Cod today. The deer have been a constant source of food for the people who have lived on the Cape for thousands of years. *Photo courtesy of Gary Clarke*

The grassy hollow cradling the old house protects it from the worst of winter's wind. And just as this placement in the landscape shelters it, the ridgepole placed east to west, positioned just so, with the front door facing south, captures the best of sunlight hours. This construction with intention tells a story of a people becoming increasingly familiar with the vagaries of the weather, seasons, and tides on the outer Cape. Today, the Atwood-Higgins House sits off Bound Brook Island Road, which—having turned from pavement to dirt—wanders away from the house in the hollow, off in a different direction into a pitch pine forest. While Cape Cod has its share of old, antique homes, the Atwood-Higgins House site, on land now protected by the Cape Cod National Seashore, offers a rare opportunity to step back in time.

The pavement of the roadway here turns to dirt, helping lend to a sense of an older era; the trees surrounding the clearing where the home sits have regrown. The landscape has filled in, making it look more like it did when colonial settlers arrived. Some of the earliest descriptions of this part of Cape Cod record a variety of trees: pine, white oak, sassafras, juniper, birch, holly, ash, and walnut. As evening falls and the light softens, the voice of the wind fills the silence. The fragrance of marsh, sun-warmed and salty, and rosa rugosa fills the air. Deer, one by one, often step out onto this quiet lawn. They are frequent visitors to this peaceful place.

The evolution of a place can be cyclical. When Thomas Higgins built the house we see, much of the land had been cleared for agricultural purposes, and erosion was a growing concern. Called Wellfleet today, the area was first home to the people of the Wampanoag nation, regionally known as Punanokanits or Nausets. A plot was farmed for a decade or so, then people moved to a new farming site when nutrients were depleted.

The earliest people of European descent to move to Wellfleet—what was then Eastham—came to Bound Brook Island in the middle of the seventeenth century. Families were drawn by salt marshes, easy access to the sea, and open land for grazing and growing. The area was so named, simply enough, because it was bound by a brook. That "brook" today winds through the deep tangle of brush that surrounds the rolling lawn in front of the house. Rapid degradation of the soil on the outer Cape, which was never good to begin with, turned residents' focus to the sea as a source of sustenance and enterprise. Roughly one hundred years later, Thomas Higgins bought the property, which had always belonged to his ancestors, for a little less than $400. While the house is tucked in a hollow, this part of Cape Cod is elevated. In Higgins's time, a soul could see ocean and bay, far out beyond the tip of the Cape to the full sweep of the horizon.

In his book chronicling his experiences walking the Cape, Henry David Thoreau wrote, "Cape Cod is the bared and bended arm of Massachusetts: the shoulder is at Buzzard's Bay; the elbow, or crazy-bone, at Cape Mallebarre; the wrist at Truro; and the sandy fist at Provincetown." To explain where they live, Cape Codders these days will still curl their arms up, as if making a muscle, and point at a spot. Thoreau's word choice of "bared" says it all. In 1602, Thomas Morton, a trader, described how people who were native to the area tended the forests here. People used fire to clear undergrowth that would impede easy travel and to create open land for agriculture. Burning also created regrowth, with new, tender shoots that helped feed deer, an important food source. Burning occurred during late fall and early spring to minimize wildfires, although large fires did occur more frequently than they do today as a result of human error and natural causes.

George Higgins, who acquired the historic home in the early twentieth century and saw to its preservation in the national park, did extensive research on the history of the site. Higgins built the other house, barn, cottage, and outbuildings during the early twentieth century, intending to create the appearance of a slightly larger complex than the actual old home. Higgins wanted it to be used as the kind of place where colonial traditions and history were preserved in a living-museum approach. Higgins wrote,

The Atwood-Higgins House is located within the boundaries of the Cape Cod National Seashore. The house has been preserved and at times is open to the public. *Photo by Susanna Graham-Pye*

> If the original homestead dates as early as 1635, the original builder not only lived among Indians, but probably lived here without permission of the Pilgrim Fathers at Plymouth the Fathers who were very jealous of their authority to grant settling on Cape Cod. Eastham itself was not settled until 1644. However, George E. Willison in the history of the Pilgrims (Saints and Strangers) Chap. XXI, says, regarding families moving to Nauset on Cape Cod in 1644 . . . the leaders in the agitation (to have their land rights respected) had already staked out fields and started buildings on the Cape, and insistently asked permission to proceed, which at length was granted.

Higgins concluded: "An old house is a constant care. Captain Atwood ran this house back to 1680 but said it was even older. Antiquarians in my 'time' have dated it 1650 minus. It was a half house before it was a whole (double) house. It once no doubt bore an outside chimney. The east half is much older than the west half."[1] References appear in area histories saying that the Atwood family enslaved people. However, some of the records in which this claim is made are based on a postrevolution census, when slavery had been abolished for close to twenty years. This could mean the Atwoods had people they'd formerly enslaved still living with and working for them.

Bound Brook Island grew. Whale-spotting towers sprouted; oysters, herring, cod, and mackerel fed the community and were shipped up and down the coast. The community built its own schoolhouse and church. Cape Cod Bay and the Atlantic Ocean offered all who lived here incomparable beauty and seemingly endless sustenance.

Today, fishing on Cape Cod Bay can be a leisurely summer pastime. Both sports fishermen and commercial fishermen still make a livelihood on the bay's waters. *Photo by Susanna Graham-Pye*

In an area where life was so sculpted by the sea, shipbuilding was added to the industries of the Cape, somewhat simultaneously with human trafficking from the colony. Prior to larger shipyards being established in towns on Cape Cod, vessels were often purchased elsewhere in the state and from other New England settlements, such as Kingston, Medford, Marblehead, Maine, and Rhode Island. The *Freemason* was the first ship built in Wellfleet sometime around 1800 at the base of the hill below the Atwood house. Within twenty short years, 357 vessels had been constructed in Wellfleet. However, long before that, Captain William Pierce—captain of the *Anne*, which brought the second load of colonists to Plymouth—had the 120-ton vessel *Desire* built for him in 1637 in Marblehead.[2] Shortly after her completion, *Desire* headed for Boston, where she was loaded with cargo and people. In a 1938 article written in the newspaper *Marblehead Messenger*, the reporter describes the scene: "One cold morning a file of soldiers tramped down the dock, escorting a stoical group of Pequot Indians who had been captured after a swamp fight at Fairfield, Conn. There were two women and fifteen boys ranging in age from 10 to fifteen years." These were not seasoned warriors, but rather women and children. The desire for young boys for the plantations of Bermuda is evident in a letter from Hugh Peter to John Winthrop. Peters wrote, "Mr. Endecot and myself salute you in the Lord Jesus, etc. Wee have heard of a dividence of women and children in the bay and would bee glad of a share, viz. : a young woman or girl and a boy if you think good. / wrote to you for some boyes for Bermudas."[3]

Whether grounded in fact or written with a touch of poetic license, the images in the *Messenger*'s article are hard, but important, to consider. The very name of the ship, *Desire*, is symbolic of the colonists' desires to succeed and flourish as a financial power in the global economy. There is nothing loving and longing in the ship's name; it was a moniker heralding covetousness and greed and power wherever she landed. The name was a statement. The *Marblehead Messenger* article described how Pierce, "knowing there was even more money to be made on negro slaves," traded one human cargo for another:

> If the trip down had been hell to the poor Indians, the trip north was even worse to the blacks for most of them were entirely without clothing and there were even more of them packed into the space in which the man of today would not even keep a dog. . . . As day after day of the voyage went by, the stench that was to distinguish the slaver in years to come, rose steaming from the hatch grating to pollute the air. As the weather grew colder, the sufferings of the poor blacks increased, for born and raised in the [tropics],

the icy winds of this northern land cut them to the bone . . . [Upon landing in Boston,] the slaves were kept ashore for a few days until their strength was recovered and then they were sold at a handsome profit to Samuel Maverick.[4]

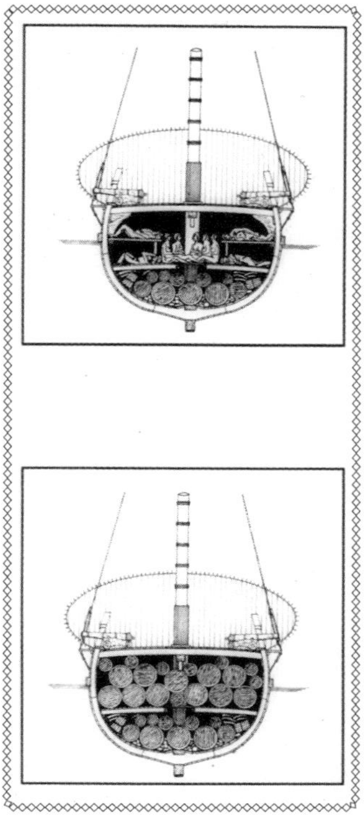

Artists' reconstruction of cross section of the hold. The top illustration depicts the ship the *Henrietta Marie* converted to carry Africans on the Middle Passage. The bottom shows the *Henrietta Marie* converted to carry cargo. The ship traveled the triangular route, moving cargo that included people who were enslaved between Europe, the West Indies, and Americas.

The *Desire* was not built as a slave ship but was made to carry cargo, such as cotton, rice, molasses, sugar, fabric, and other items. Ships such as the *Whydah*, however, built in England and elsewhere in Europe, were specifically designed for trafficking large numbers of people. *Whydah* was a galley, a square-rigged, three-masted vessel. *Whydah* was 110 feet long, with a 300-ton rating. It could travel up to 13 knots and was armed with cannons on the deck. New Englanders, on the other hand, preferred using schooners. Because schooners were faster than larger, heavier vessels, they moved between destinations more quickly, cutting down on the number of deaths among the people intended for enslavement. The shallow draft of schooners made the boats good both for shallow waters around ports in Africa and up and down the Eastern Seaboard of colonial North America (later the United States of America).

Sloops were also used in trade between the West Indies and New England ports. Slightly smaller, and with Bermuda rigging versus schooners' two-masted gaff rigging, the boats were sleek and fast. In 1764, Eleazar Atwood had a sloop built for him in Kingston, Massachusetts.[5] He named his ship *Wellfleet*. The 60-ton vessel was used by the Atwoods for the trading business, most likely for coastal work between the colonies. Shortly after its completion, according to records in the slavevoyages.org database, captain John Atwood "departed an American Port with slaves." The "principal place where slaves were purchased" is listed as Boston. The people who were enslaved "disembarked in the Americas" in an unspecified port in North Carolina. In 1773, an Atwood, with no first name noted as

This heart-shaped lock hangs on the door of one of the buildings at the Atwood-Higgins complex in Wellfleet. *Photo by Susanna Graham-Pye*

owner or captain on the ship, is recorded in this way: "Particular outcome of the voyage: slaves sold." The record also says the people enslaved were transported from Dominica to Charleston.[6]

Common sense, the rules of economics, and what history is recorded allow us to piece together the confidence to assert that Cape Cod's maritime industry, in more than one way, was inextricably chained to chattel slavery. If, indeed, hundreds of boats were built in Wellfleet and hundreds were constructed in other areas of the peninsula, they were used to move "goods" between West Indian islands; at times Africa, Europe, and the Americas; and up and down the coast. Salt was produced on Cape Cod to preserve cod, cod was used to feed the people who were enslaved, and those people were the ones who grew the sugar, which made the molasses used to create the rum traded for more people. It was a cycle at the heart of which the Cape's mariners worked.

Places for Reflection
WELLFLEET

ATWOOD-HIGGINS HOUSE

269 Bound Brook Island Road, Wellfleet
41.95989275087791, −70.05907156112625

Once truly an island, Bound Brook Island today is a neighborhood in Wellfleet, part Cape Cod National Seashore, part private homes. The home itself is owned by the Seashore and, at times during the past, has been open to the public. The main home is a colonial-era original, while the outbuildings were built by George Higgins in the 1930s. Higgins had a vision of creating a historical-reproduction farm that people could visit. Those buildings have fallen into disrepair. The property is a lovely place to step back through the portal of time, to listen to the wind in the trees.

MARCONI BEACH

Marconi Beach Road, Wellfleet
41.89317174373784, −69.96164705301003

Marconi Beach, on the ocean side of Wellfleet, is so named for Guglielmo Marconi, an inventor who worked to prove that wireless transmissions could be made across the Atlantic Ocean. A message was sent between the president of the United States and the king of England in January 1903 from a station located near today's beach and visitor center. The wreck of the Whydah was found off Marconi Beach. The beach is one of the beautiful ocean beaches protected by the Cape Cod National Seashore.

CHAPTER 10

Truro—Abolition

“WUTHERING” BEING A SIGNIFICANT PROVINCIAL ADJECTIVE, DESCRIPTIVE OF THE ATMOSPHERIC TUMULT TO WHICH ITS STATION IS EXPOSED IN STORMY WEATHER. PURE, BRACING VENTILATION THEY MUST HAVE UP THERE AT ALL TIMES, INDEED; ONE MAY GUESS THE POWER OF THE NORTH WIND BLOWING OVER THE EDGE, BY THE EXCESSIVE SLANT OF A FEW-STUNTED FIRS AT THE END OF THE HOUSE; AND BY A RANGE OF GAUNT THORNS ALL STRETCHING THEIR LIMBS ONE WAY, AS IF CRAVING ALMS OF THE SUN.

—EMILY BRONTË,
Wuthering Heights

Pamet Hill offers an expansive view of the ocean and the dunes. At once beautiful and desolate, the landscape is ever changing but, somehow, always the same. *Photo courtesy of Ryan Johnson*

There is indeed something of *Wuthering Heights* in Truro's landscape. Just as the moors of the book's fictional landscape symbolize the spaces that lie between good and evil, life and death, Truro's Pamet Hills are a captivating and moving landscape: literally, as the winds sweep off the ocean and constantly resculpt the landscape, and figuratively, for those looking out over the hills—a place where dune grasses trace delicate circles in purple shadows—can't help but have their emotions in the moment exaggerated and deepened. Little about the sweep of sand and wind or the dune grass would make any soul kidnapped and trafficked into slavery feel at home here. Standing atop the Pamet Hills, the vastness of the ocean is inescapable. The arc of the horizon—absent interruption from any of the lands we know to be faraway—makes clear how apart we are, and how alone we can be. For one who survived transport through the Middle Passage, that hauntingly enormous, inescapable view of the Atlantic from Pamet Hills must have been a brutal daily reminder of one's enslavement. The dunes on this narrowing strip of sand are a powerful place to stand and acknowledge those who were enslaved here.

For the most part, as little as fifty or so years ago, recognition of New England's enormous role in the trafficking of humans appears only here and there. While some information can be found in scholarly articles and academic research, not much was offered in popular culture or classrooms. Until very recently, if it was acknowledged at all that the institution of slavery existed in the North, it was done in quaint terms that depicted lives of enslavement as far better in the North than in the South, as in this description written by Alice Morse Earle in 1893 in her *Customs and Fashions in Old New England*:

> In the main, New England slaves were not unhappy, for they were well treated, and the race has the gift to be merry in the worst of circumstances. Occasionally one would be brought to the northern land, one of higher sensibilities, more sensitive affections, greater pride; one who could not live a slave. Such a one was the haughty Congo Pomp, who escaped to a swamp near Truro on Cape Cod—a swamp now called by his name—and placing at the foot of a tree a jug of water and loaf of bread to sustain him on his last long journey, hanged himself from the low-hanging limbs, and thus obtained freedom.[1]

Rather than being temperamental, haughty, or oversensitive, too filled with pride to live as a slave, Pomp likely felt what Harriet Tubman explained: "I had reasoned this out in my mind: there was one of two things I had a right to, liberty, or death; if I could not have one, I would have the other."

This lithograph shows a man who was born in the Congo. His name was Kangga; he was baptized in Jamaica as Louis but was called Lovey.

Describing the same occurrence of Pomp's suicide, Oliver Knowles pens a more realistic picture in a 1948 *Cape Codder* newspaper article, writing, "Pomp . . . probably hastened the abolition of slavery on the Cape when he hung himself in his frenzied loneliness." And author Shebnah Rich elaborates, offering details of Pomp's death in his 1883 book *Truro—Cape Cod*, saying Pomp, "an African of the pure Congo species," believed in metempsychosis, or the transmigration of the soul, and suffered from "homesick passion." Today, Pomps Lot Road in Truro is a subdivision of year-round and summer homes.[2]

For the growing number of us beginning to understand and

grapple with all that has been unremembered in the pages of history, who know the reality of the Civil War, Reconstruction, the civil rights movement, and the people—thousands of them—who were lynched between the end of the Civil War and the beginning of World War II, it's hard not to ask if Pomp hanged himself, or if he was hanged. Unfortunately, but realistically, it's easier to picture a world in which Pomp, taking food and water for his trip, was caught trying to escape and was murdered in retaliation for his attempt. Hypotheticals aside, Pomp undoubtedly died due to his enslavement, and many, many people who were enslaved, unable to find physical freedom, opted for a metaphysical route and took their own lives.

We won't ever know the specifics. However, the romanticized telling in Rich's book was published only thirteen years after the passage of the Fifteenth Amendment to the Constitution, which closed many of the legal loopholes that abetted efforts of repression in the Jim Crow South. Perhaps early accounts of Pomp's death that Rich read in his research were a carefully crafted propaganda meant to tug at the heartstrings of a northern population increasingly opposed to chattel slavery. During a time when the call for abolition was at its highest, Rich was looking back at a prerevolutionary period when the enslavement of people in Massachusetts was at its height. He wrote from the vantage of a post–Civil War Northerner. Here, the original factors contributing to the Civil War, the initial involvement of the northern colonies and later states in the creation and maintenance of the chattel slave industry, were obscured by the war, which was increasingly presented as one fought solely over slavery: North versus South, slavery or none. Out of this period of Reconstruction, the North wrote its history in a way that downplayed—and even, in many cases, erased—its role in the origin story of enslavement in the nation.

Moving into the latter half of the eighteenth century, as people increasingly pointed out the absurdity of enslavement existing alongside calls for liberty and equality, Massachusetts became the first to abolish slavery completely. Other states—Vermont and Pennsylvania, for example—had successfully begun a phased approach to abolition earlier. Like underlying factors of the Civil War, this measure was as much pragmatic and political as it was moral. The economy was suffering, coastal trade would be disrupted during the Revolutionary War, and Massachusetts did not rely on slave labor or its economic successes as much as other colonies in the South. Years after Massachusetts made slavery illegal, John Adams argued that the real justification for the abolition of slavery in Massachusetts had in fact been driven by the growing number of working white people "who would no longer suffer the Rich to employ these Sable Rivals, so much to their Injury." [And that] "if the Gentlemen [versus a working class] had been permitted by Law to hold Slaves," he says, "the common white People would have put the Negroes to Death and their Masters too perhaps." White laborers, scoffing at and insulting, "filled the Negroes with Discontent," making them "wholly useless to their Masters: to such a degree that the abolition of slavery became a Measure of Oeconomy."[3] Adams's comments were made in response to a request from Judge St. George Tucker of Virginia, who wrote to Jeremy Belknap of Boston. Tucker, a law professor at the College of William & Mary, asked Belknap to gather comments in an effort to learn how Massachusetts had achieved abolition so peacefully. Belknap passed the letters on to a number of the commonwealth's leaders. That collection is held at the Massachusetts Historical Society, of which Belknap was a founder.

In the same series of letters, James Winthrop wrote a response for Belknap in 1795. After outlining the various steps toward abolition the state had taken, he noted,

> I do not recollect any thing further on this subject, but I cannot forbear adding, that it would be more worthy of an enlightened Legislature to regulate a trade that is woven into our nature, and has been carried on, and considered as lawful from the earliest antiquity, than try to abolish it. If abuses have crept in, they should be guarded against: but abuse alone will not justify abolishing a trade which manifestly tends to preserve life and increase the quantity of productive labor in the whole world.

As far from moral arguments against slavery as Winthrop and others might have been, Massachusetts had its share of those who opposed slavery and spoke out against the institution for moral reasons. Elihu Coleman, a Quaker minister on Nantucket, was among the first in Massachusetts and the colonies to take a public stance against slavery. In 1733, publishing "A Testimony against the Anti-Christian Practice of Making Slaves of Men," Coleman systematically refuted many claims made using biblical passages to defend slavery. In a straightforward, simple contemplation, Coleman asks his readers: "Now, if anyone should ask one of the negroe's masters that had a negro child and a child of his own, what harm one had done, that it should be made more a slave than the other, they would not be able to answer it." To make one child a slave over another, Coleman argues, is not only "against scripture" but against nature.

Another Cape Codder, James Otis, was born in West Barnstable and moved to Boston, where he served as a representative in the General Assembly. He spoke out strongly against slavery. In 1764 he pointed out the incongruity of fighting for liberty alongside the practice of enslaving people in his "Rights of the British Colonies Asserted and Proved." In the document, he called slavery "the most shocking violation of the law of nature" and pointed out that current rhetoric about natural rights for freedom conflicted with chattel slavery.[4]

Beginning in the 1760s and until the first "shot heard round the world" was fired in 1775, town meetings across Massachusetts passed resolutions urging their representatives to create legislation to ban the importation of slaves. In 1773, Sandwich joined other towns throughout the state, passing resolutions supporting natural rights and calling for an end to slavery. That same year, Ezra Stiles, the president of Yale University, along with other religious leaders, suggested creating a colony in West Africa for people freed from enslavement, and to stop the importation of slaves. A group of people enslaved in Massachusetts petitioned the court for freedom. Massachusetts's General Assembly made several attempts to ban the importation of slaves, but those efforts were shot down by the colonial governor. After the American Revolution, Massachusetts adopted its constitution in 1780, which contained this Declaration of Human Rights: "All people are born free and equal and have certain natural, essential and unalienable rights; among which may be reckoned the right of enjoying and defending their lives and liberties; that of acquiring, possessing and protecting property; in fine, that of seeking and obtaining their safety and happiness."[5]

Prior to Massachusetts's adoption of its constitution, most legal cases and appeals to higher courts in Massachusetts—where people were both enslaved by law and protected as individuals under the law—dealt with specific breaches of law. For example, a number of cases dealt with unkept promises of freedom or questions about the legitimacy of one's enslavement due to birth circumstances. People's legal fights took a sharp philosophical turn almost immediately after Massachusetts adopted its constitution. In 1781, in *Brom and Bett v. Ashley*, Theodore Sedgwick, a Deerfield attorney, argued on behalf of Brom and Bett, a man and woman enslaved in the Ashley household in western Massachusetts. He posited the notion that the Massachusetts Constitution made slavery illegal. The court agreed. While it is unclear what happened to Brom, Mum Bett, who legally changed her name to Elizabeth Freeman, went on to work for the Sedgwick family as a domestic servant. Sedgwick's daughter, Catharine Maria Sedgwick, wrote a biography about Freeman's life. Far from the quaint picture painted in Alice Morse Earle's book, where good-natured people of African descent had a life of relative ease compared to southern slaves, the realities of Freeman's life of enslavement were captured by Sedgwick in passages such as this:

Bet interposed her brawny arm & took the blow—It cut quite across the arm to the bone—"but," she would say afterwards in concluding the story of the frightful scar she carried to her grave Madam never again laid her hand on Lirry—I had a bad arm all winter but Madam had the worst of it—I never covered the wound, & when people said to me before Madam—"Why Betty! what ails your arm," I only answered, "ask Missess"!—Which was the slave, & which the real mistress?[6]

Elizabeth Freeman, known during the time she was enslaved by a family in western Massachusetts as Mum Bett, petitioned the Massachusetts courts for her freedom. Her case is considered a significant turning point that helped with the abolition of slavery in Massachusetts.

The other significant case that brought about the abolition of slavery in Massachusetts was Quock Walker's case. What began as a suit by Walker for his freedom because of promises made and broken by his enslavers ultimately was decided on the basis of the new constitution. Quock's case was first denied but ultimately played out in his favor in the Massachusetts Supreme Court—long before the fledgling country's Supreme Court established the concept of judicial review with *Marbury v. Madison*. In Quock's case, Supreme Judicial Court chief justice William Cushing announced that slavery was incompatible with the new Massachusetts Constitution:

These sentiments [that are favorable to the natural rights of mankind] led the framers of our constitution of government—by which the people of this commonwealth have solemnly bound themselves to each other—to declare—that all men are born free and equal; and that every subject is entitled to liberty, and to have it guarded by the laws as well as his life and property. In short, without resorting to implication in constructing the constitution, slavery is in my judgment as effectively abolished as it can be by the granting of rights and privileges wholly incompatible and repugnant to its existence. The court are therefore fully of the opinion that perpetual servitude can no longer be tolerated in our government, and that liberty can only be forfeited by some criminal conduct or relinquished by personal

> consent or contract. And it is therefore unnecessary to consider whether the promises of freedom to Quaco, on the part of his master and mistress, amounted to a manumission or not.

Pennsylvania banned the importation of slaves before any other state; Massachusetts was the first to completely abolish slavery. However, freedom did not amount to anything resembling equality. The social status of people of African descent, formerly enslaved, was perhaps somewhat higher than those still living in enslavement elsewhere in the newly independent country, but only slightly. The lives of "freed" people in Massachusetts were legally restricted in many ways: people of African descent could not entertain or gather, they could not own swine, nor could they carry sticks (unless those sticks were needed for walking). Interracial marriage was banned. People of African descent were required to pay taxes but were not allowed to vote; most children did not attend school. Jobs for "freed" people were extremely limited, and in communities where maritime trades dominated the labor market, people were reluctant to work on docks or ships where a return to slavery in other parts of the country was likely. In 1788, the Constitution was ratified, but the importation of slaves was not banned nationwide for another twenty years. Even though the 1808 federal law prohibited international chattel slavery, more than 3.5 million people were born into slavery in America. Children were sold away from parents, families were broken apart, and people were traded throughout the country in what was the largest forced migration in American history.

Various publications about Cape Cod written during the earlier part of the twentieth century mention people who were enslaved in Truro. There were Joe, Violet, Dinah, Pomp, and Hector, who holds the title "the last slave." Unlike Pomp, Hector was born into slavery in Truro, then sold at the age of three. Lieutenant Jonathan Paine of Truro was reported to have enslaved numerous people. One of them was Joe, who "arrived at middle age." Whether this means Joe arrived in Truro or the colonies when he was middle-aged isn't clear. The story goes on to say that Joe told Paine he wanted a wife, at which suggestion "his kind-hearted master promised his influence and, faithful as kind, when he next visited Boston he returned with a mate for his servant." The woman was described as "ugly as the furies and black as Erebus." The couple gave birth to a son, Hector, who was sold to Benjamin Collins for thirty pounds in 1726 when the child was three years old. Collins was said to have hundreds of acres in Truro where he grew primarily corn but also wheat, oats, and flax. Hector was baptized in his twenties in 1747 by Reverend John Avery and is identified in the church records as the "slave of Benjamin Collins." Hector tended Collins's livestock and worked on Collins's farm until his death. He was reported often to be overheard praying to himself as he worked.

A talk given by Joshua Dyer at the Truro Lyceum was the source of much of the information used in Rich's book to describe Hector. He quotes Dyer at length:

> There are those living now who remember Hector, an old man with bleached locks and dim eyes, struggling amid the last waves of a toilsome life. He sighed not for Africa. Truro was his home and he knew no other. During a long life he had scarce wandered beyond the bounds of his lowing herds, or the meanderings of the Pamet which he paddled so often in his little canoe."[7]

The passage creates a pastoral tableau of Hector's life, like Thomas Cole's painting titled *Old Age*, in his Voyage of Life series of paintings.

If readers of Rich's work struggled to comprehend the existence of chattel slavery in New England, a place filled with souls of "positive conscience and honest convictions," he urges them to consider that "not thirty years are yet passed since slavery was defended by the press, the pulpit, the platform and the sword of this Christian nation. The villainous traffic in African slaves was prosecuted with great energy and profit and regarded a fair field for enterprise for more than 100 years after the settlement of Plymouth."[8] Could Rich have imagined the struggles that still exist today as the nation continues to respond to the fallout of more than two centuries of the government-sponsored enslavement of so many people?

Old Age in the series Voyage of Life, oil on canvas, was painted in 1842 by Thomas Cole and is one of a series depicting the various stages of life. Interpretations of the artist's intent vary, and rightfully so. Information at the National Museum in Washington, DC, where the paintings are housed, suggests, "The artist may have been issuing a dire warning . . . that unbridled westward expansion and industrialization would have tragic consequences for both man and nature." *Photo courtesy of the Alisa Mellon Bruce Fund*

Places for Reflection

TRURO

BENJAMIN COLLINS HOUSE AND THE PAMET HILLS

South Pamet Road, Truro
41.99624784240805, –70.02582037459341

At times in the past, the old house, one of the first built in Truro, has been referred to as "home to Hector, Truro's last slave." Hector was enslaved by Benjamin Collins. He was born in Truro and died in Truro. The home is a lovely example of a classic double Cape Cod home. It is a private home today, not open to the public. However, a drive down South Pamet Road provides a meandering ride through the beautiful Pamet Hills, a landscape familiar to Hector and the others who lived their lives in enslavement in Truro.

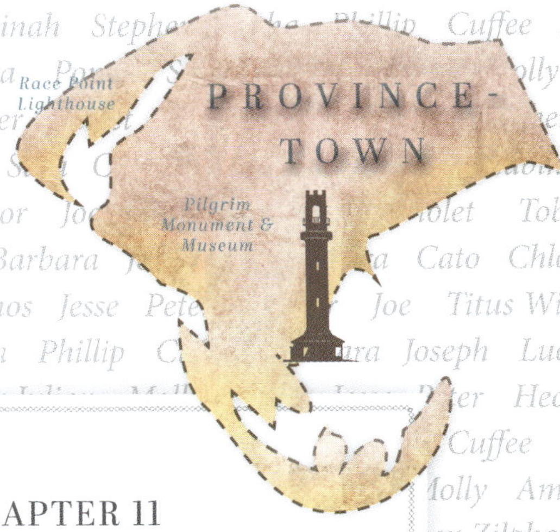

CHAPTER 11

Provincetown to Bourne—Full Circle

ENDS AND BEGINNINGS—THERE ARE NO SUCH THINGS. THERE ARE ONLY MIDDLES.

—ROBERT FROST

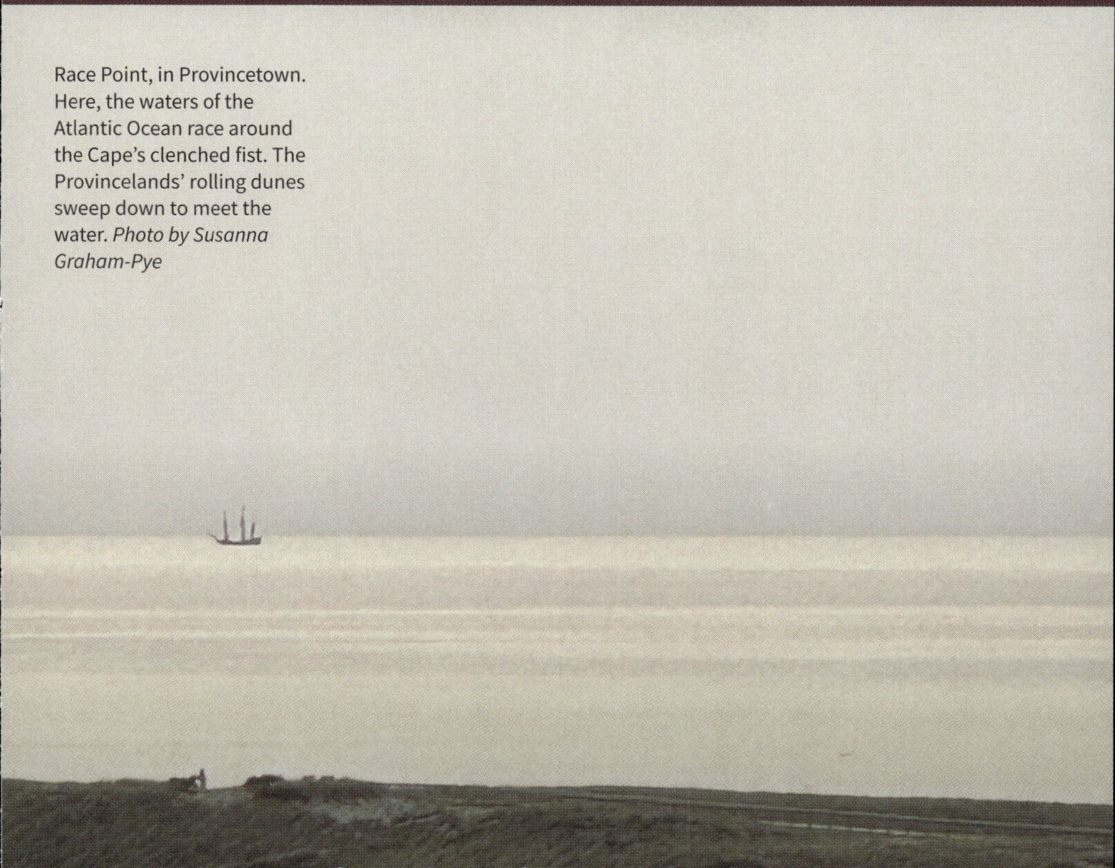

Race Point, in Provincetown. Here, the waters of the Atlantic Ocean race around the Cape's clenched fist. The Provincelands' rolling dunes sweep down to meet the water. *Photo by Susanna Graham-Pye*

Like a beckoning finger, the tip of Provincetown curls around Cape Cod Bay—an ever-changing surface of reflection, broken by wind-whipped whitecaps, the shattered light of brilliant sunsets, diving seafaring birds, whales, and dolphins. The bay is the ever presence around which this peninsula's history has been built, skipping like a smooth beach stone from period to period and by a people using it in different, but oddly similar, ways.

The very tip of Cape Cod, what we call Provincetown today and was known as Meeshawn to the Indigenous people, marks the northern boundary of what is sometimes translated as Dawnland, home to the people of Wampanoag descent, People of the First Light. The area stretches southward to Narragansett Bay and is home to an estimated sixty-nine tribes of the Wampanoag people—an ironic geography considering Massachusetts's and Rhode Island's dual role as leaders in the early colonies' participation in the trafficking of hundreds of thousands of people from Africa to the West Indies and Americas. That trafficking began first when Captain William Pierce brought settlers to join the others at Plymouth . . . the Merchant Adventurers from the Dutch Leiden across the Atlantic Ocean. Pierce went on to captain the ships that brought the founders of Massachusetts Bay Colony. In classrooms in New England, little attention is given to the captain of the ship who brought the colonists here. Even less to the fact that Pierce turned his attention to making the colonies and himself great financial successes and was among the first to begin moving kidnapped people indigenous to New England to trade for people of African descent.

When the people of Provincetown petitioned the colonial powers to become a town, they asked to be called Herringtown. The government rejected the request, giving it the name of Provincetown. Meeshawn, Herringtown, Helltown, P-town—call it what you will, the shifting sands have always cradled the people here on the edges of the rich waters that race around the tip of land. It is suspected that on the night his ship went down, Captain Samuel Bellamy was headed for Helltown, so called because of the pirates who stopped there in their travels; it is the place spotted by Pilgrims who were driven off course to arrive here instead of in Virginia in 1620.

In 1907, President Theodore Roosevelt laid the first stone for construction of the Pilgrim Monument, but the association that spearheaded the idea for the structure was founded in 1892. The Roosevelt family was not known to enslave people, but the president's mother, Martha Bulloch Roosevelt, grew up in Savannah, Georgia, where her father was a partner in a cotton mill. The family enslaved as many as thirty-three people, who did the work that built the family's wealth. Some speculate that "Mittie," as the wealthy socialite was known, served as fodder for Margaret Mitchell's creation of the character Scarlett O'Hara in the novel *Gone with the Wind*. That Roosevelt, given his ancestry, laid the cornerstone of the monument is heavily symbolic of the nation's tangled roots.

The president arrived on a beautiful summer day in August—169 years, almost to the day, after Jean, the woman discussed in chapter 1 at the beginning of our journey, was sold to a new enslaver and left her home in Sandwich—the young, pregnant woman moving to live in Plymouth, America's so-called hometown founded by the Pilgrims that Roosevelt commemorated. His speech, a long one, was part of a longer ceremony during which Masonic rituals punctuated proceedings. In part, with words that in some ways could apply to current events, Roosevelt said,

> The Puritan's task was to conquer a continent; not merely to overrun it, but to settle it, to till it, to build upon it a high industrial and social life; and, while engaged in the rough work of taming the shaggy wilderness, at that very time also to lay deep the immovable foundations of our whole American system of civil, political, and religious liberty achieved through the orderly process of law. This was the work allotted him to do; this is the work he did; and only a master spirit among men could have done it. . . . We have traveled far since his day. That liberty of conscience which he demanded for himself, we now

realize must be as freely accorded to others as it is resolutely insisted upon for ourselves. The splendid qualities which he left to his children, we other Americans who are not of Puritan blood also claim as our heritage. You, sons of the Puritans, and we, who are descended from races whom the Puritans would have deemed alien—we are all Americans together. We all feel the same pride in the genesis, in the history, of our people; and therefore this shrine of Puritanism is one at which we all gather to pay homage, no matter from what country our ancestors sprang. . . . There exists no more sordid and unlovely type of social development than a plutocracy, for there is a peculiar unwholesomeness in a social and governmental ideal where wealth by and of itself is held up as the greatest good. The materialism of such a view, whether it finds its expression in the life of a man who accumulates a vast fortune in ways that are repugnant to every instinct of generosity and of fair dealing, or whether it finds its expression in the vapidly useless and self-indulgent life of the inheritor of that fortune, is contemptible in the eyes of all men capable of a thrill of lofty feeling.[1]

They were prophetic words rooted deeply in the reality of a nation built upon a powerful elite made rich—some would argue almost entirely—upon the stolen lives of millions of people who were enslaved.

It takes 116 steps to reach the top of the Pilgrim Monument in Provincetown. The effort is rewarded with sweeping views of Cape Cod Bay and the land that cradles it. *Photo by Susanna Graham-Pye*

Among the towns of Cape Cod, Provincetown has been the only one for which finding at least one reference to a person who was enslaved by a family in the town is difficult. Incorporated in 1727—a point when New England was firmly entrenched in the business of human trafficking and the region's shipmasters were among the leaders at moving enslaved people in the triangular trade route—Provincetown, for the moment, remains a mystery. Perhaps this is because Provincetown ship owners and captains worked so much in whaling, and whaling in New England was dominated by Quakers, who did not believe in the enslavement of people.

In a lovely column published in the *Cape Cod Times* nearly thirty years ago, Wellfleet's Betty Burkes recalled a conversation she'd had with George Bryant, who worked in town and county politics representing the people of Provincetown. Bryant recounted his own chats with an old-timer in town, Warren Silva, who could remember going down to the docks in the late 1800s to watch the ships come and go. Burkes quotes Bryant, who quotes Silva, saying, "When I was boy, most of the men on the whaling ships were colored." These people who worked whaling were primarily from the West Indies. Like on pirate ships, where many were given freedom in exchange for allegiance to captains, on whaling ships, many captains granted people who were enslaved their freedom as well—though certainly many were enslaved by captains too. As the plantation systems of the West Indies began to falter in the latter part of the nineteenth century, many people in the islands turned their attention to harvesting whales from the oceans that surrounded them. It is estimated that only a handful of men of African descent became captains of whaling ships; Provincetown claims two of them. Captain Colin Stevenson was a native of St. Vincent, captained a ship in the Provincetown whaling fleet, and ultimately settled in town. He was captain of the *Rising Sun*, *Alcyone*, and *Carrie D. Knowles*. The other known whaler of African descent out of Provincetown was William T. Shorey, who came to Provincetown from Barbados in 1876 to work for Samuel S. Swift. Shorey went on to live on and sail off the West Coast. It is nice to think that Provincetown was, as it continues to be, a singular town that bucked

Nile was born in 1987. She is known for getting quite close to whale watch boats. *Photo by Carolyn O'Connor*

Hovering just below the surface, this six-month-old humpback checks out the visitors. Look closely and you can see the curiosity in her eye, peering up at the boat. *Photo by Carolyn O'Connor*

popular trends. This, however, is unlikely. At some point, it seems inevitable that someone will find a record bearing the words "my negro" related to someone who lived in Provincetown.

Today, the whales that come to the coast continue to offer a livelihood to the people of Cape Cod. Harvesting whales has turned to watching whales. The Dolphin Fleet, launched by one of the Cape's oldest fishing families when the fishing industry began to falter, offers visitors and year-rounders passage out to Georges Bank. There, people may observe the profound interactions between whales and the waters in which they live.

The Province Lands visitor center now sits within the Cape Cod National Seashore on land once known as Nigger Head. That name changed on maps in the early to mid-1900s to Negro Head. The origin of the name is not clear but perhaps is related to the number of mariners working in Provincetown who were of African descent. Today, the visitor center offers a beautiful view from which visitors can contemplate the history of this land.

When the Pilgrim Monument Association began its planning for its 252-foot-tall tower, the harbor still offered a berth to whaling ships. When Roosevelt arrived for the groundbreaking celebration, the whaling industry was on its last legs.

From the top of the monument today on a clear day, visitors who climb the 116 steps in the tallest granite structure in the US can look back at where our story began, in Sandwich, where the first people enslaved on Cape Cod were recorded—at least the first enslaved by people of European descent who migrated to these shores. Looking back, just behind Sandwich and the canal, lies Bourne, the last region to become a town here, breaking from Sandwich in 1884. Bourne, where Aptucxet Trading Post first struck up business with peoples from around the world, was perhaps the Cape's only industrial boomtown. Saltworks and gristmills gave way to ironworks in Bournedale and Cohasset. Construction of the canal, however, sealed the death certificate of those enterprises when they were cut off from the mainland.

Bourne is the only town on the Cape to become a town when the practice of enslavement was finally illegal. However, this is not to say that enslavement was not a part of its beginnings too. Bourne is named for Richard Bourne, one of the "Ten Men of Saugus," probably related to Jonathan Bourne, who enslaved Jean. In the inventory of Richard's estate, "one servant" is listed among his possessions. Today, Bourne includes regions, called villages, including Bourne Village, Bournedale, Buzzards Bay, Cataumet, Gray Gables, Monument Beach, Pocasset, Sagamore, and Sagamore Beach. But the ground beneath each of these places is the land on which walked Canootus, Syman, and Joell—people indigenous to Sandwich whose ancestors had lived here for as many as 10,000 years before Richard Bourne's arrival. It was a home to Jean, enslaved by Jonathan Bourne. It was home to Bashua, whose enslaver Desire Parker gave to her daughter Rebecca Nye "my negro girl called Bashua."

From here, the names of many people have gone unmentioned, uncelebrated, in the histories of towns on the rest of Cape Cod. As the research for this book was being conducted, however, people—one by one, here and there—revealed themselves:

Zilpha

Phillip

Cuffee

Barbara

Joseph

Luce

Sara

Cato

Chloe

Sara

Pomp

Sabina

John Julian

Molly

Amos

Jesse

Peter

Hector

Joe

Titus Winchester

Violet

Toby

Bess

Dinah

Stephen

There are many other people mentioned in legal documents that rarely make it to public view—listed simply as "my negro," "negro boy," "negro girl," "negroes," "servant girl," "mulatto," "Indian." An example of such a document is the will of Captain Lothrop, a selectman and constable in the town of Barnstable, which mentions "three negroes." Or the estate inventory of Captain John Hawes, which references "two negro girls valued at £41" and an "Indian boy valued at £5." People are listed in inventories alongside pepper and indigo, barrels and bedding, silver or pewter, and land. They are listed as property, even though all—and likely many others—lived here, worked here, and contributed to survival successes that created these towns and states that ultimately became a country. Undoubtedly, if we continue to look, commit to looking, many more people can be found and remembered.

Places for Reflection

LOOKING BACK FROM PROVINCETOWN OVER TO BOURNE

RACE POINT / PROVINCE LANDS VISITOR CENTER

42.07420213650831, -70.20521840762726

Race Point is the sandy tip of the Cape. At times, whales are visible from the beach's sandy shoreline. While rare North Atlantic right whales pass offshore, humpbacks, finbacks, and minke whales come in closer to land. The Province Lands Visitors Center, open May through October, offers a variety of exhibits and movies that highlight the area's nature and history. Ranger-led hikes and activities depart from the center.

PILGRIM MONUMENT AND PROVINCETOWN MUSEUM

42.07420213650831, -70.20521840762726

President Theodore Roosevelt laid the cornerstone for the 252-foot-tall monument built to commemorate the landing of the Pilgrims who first arrived in North America on the shores of Cape Cod Bay. The ship Mayflower, which carried the adventurers from England and Holland, moored in the bay for five weeks while small expeditions were made, exploring the Cape for potential homesites. Ultimately, the group moved on to found Plymouth Bay Colony. From the top of the monument lies a magnificent, sweeping view of Cape Cod Bay. On clear days, viewers can see clear across to the power plant at the mouth of the Cape Cod Canal.

APTUCXET TRADING POST / MUSEUMS AT APTUCXET

4 Aptucxet Road, Bourne
41.74211609898618, -70.60496900344272

The Aptucxet Trading Post re-creates the trading post that was constructed by Plymouth Colony in 1627. The post was a center for trade between the local people of Wampanoag descent and the Dutch fur traders traveling throughout the area. The museum helps visitors understand the mercantile desires and endeavors of the merchant adventurers who moved to British colonies throughout the northern and southern Atlantic.

Epilogue

I have no doubt I barely touched the hazy grime covering the window into Cape Cod's past. In what wills and estate summaries I did find and examine from the seventeenth and eighteenth centuries for Cape Codders, references to enslaved people appeared more often than not. As I mention in the introduction, there are people working to locate as many of those records of people who were enslaved as they can. It is a mighty task that will take thousands of hours of work from many people. My initial intention was to see if I might find some people, and I found many. I chose several people or situations to serve as representatives of what I know to be a larger population, and whose circumstances give us an access point to the larger historical setting. I hope to continue combing through diaries, wills, and letters to find more information about the people I've identified, and I hope others will as well.

The story of enslavement and human trafficking is not over. It never really ended. Today, at any given time, worldwide, an estimated 27.6 million people are being trafficked, according to the United States Department of State. The State Department's website goes on to explain that traffickers prey on people of "all ages and backgrounds and nationalities." People who are trafficked, sold, used, enslaved—call it what you will—are done so for profit. Commercial sex, hospitality, traveling sales, agriculture, restaurants, factories, healthcare, domestic work, salons, fishing, and construction are among the primary areas in which enslavers use the labor of people whom they enslave. The United Nations estimates that 49.6 million people are enslaved, counting forced marriages.

Reflections in an old window in one of the buildings at the Atwood-Higgins House complex in the Cape Cod National Seashore. *Photo by Susanna Graham-Pye*

Acknowledgments

Thank you to my friends and family who listened to my stories as I made discovery after discovery. Thank you to Therese Gordon, my intrepid partner in searching out sites where people who were enslaved once walked. She wandered through cemeteries with me, reading dozens of gravestones in search of the burial sites of people who were enslaved here on Cape Cod. We didn't find any. She encouraged me every step of the way.

Thanks to Melissa Murphy, a member of the reference staff team at the Baker Library Special Collections and Archives at Harvard Business School; John Cullity of the Nye Homestead and Museum both for his tour of the house and honesty about grappling with his emotions upon learning his ancestors had enslaved someone; David Wright, curator at the Wellfleet Historical Society Museum; Joanie Gearin, archivist at the National Archives at Boston; Colleen Hurter, archivist at Woods Hole Historical Museum; Meg Costello, research manager at Museums on the Green; Susanna Sigler at the Massachusetts Historical Society; Jessy Wheeler of the Research Services Department at the Boston Public Library; Deborah M. Rich, town archivist and reference librarian at the Sandwich Public Library; Liz Fort at the Historical Society of Old Yarmouth; Gabrielle Faria-Kalkanis at Sturgis Library; Linda Rand at Plimoth Patuxet Museums; Judy Cunniff, archivist at the Chatham Historical Society; Donna Curtin, executive director of Pilgrim Hall Museum; Sally Gunning and Teresa Lamperti of the Brewster Historical Society; Dave Talbott at Dennis Historical Society; and Lynne Rhodes, for taking time and giving thought to reading this work and sharing her insight.

Thank you to Ryan Johnson, friend and colleague, for sharing his beautiful photography; to all who shared pictures, including Carolyn O'Connor, Gary Clarke, Allison Graham, Zukhra Graham, and Cape Cod Life Publications; and to the other museums and organizations who shared resources.

Notes

CHAPTER 1
Sandwich—Beginnings

1. Proceedings from the Records of the Colony of New Plymouth in New England, printed by order of the legislature of the commonwealth of Massachusetts, 270.
2. This text is in the public domain. The portion of it here was accessed at "Massachusetts Body of Liberties (1641)," *Learning for Justice*, https://www.learningforjustice.org/classroom-resources/texts/hard-history/massachusetts-body-of-liberties.
3. Emmanuel Downing to John Winthrop, ca. August 1645, in Allyn B. Forbes, the Winthrop Papers (Boston: Massachusetts Historical Society, 1947), 5.38–39.
4. *Beyond the Pilgrim Story—Long Road to Freedom* (n.d.), Pilgrim Hall Museum, retrieved July 28, 2023, from https://pilgrimhall.org/long_road_to_freedom.htm.
5. Alice Morse Earle, *Home Life in Colonial Days*, Internet Archive, 2017 (originally published in 1898), https://archive.org/details/in.ernet.dli.2015.233561.
6. Ibid.

CHAPTER 2
Yarmouth—Triangle

1. Mary W. Helms, "Miskito Slaving and Culture Contact: Ethnicity and Opportunity in an Expanding Population," *Journal of Anthropological Research* 39, no. 2 (1983): 179–97, https://www.jstor.org/stable/3629966.
2. Bernard Nietschmann, "The Miskito Nation and the Geopolitics of Self-Determination," *Journal of Political Science* 19, no. 1 (1991): 3, https://digitalcommons.coastal.edu/jops/vol19/iss1/3.
3. Rufus Clemens Porter, "American Merchant Shipping: A Recurring National Dilemma," *Naval War College Review* 15, no. 3 (1962): 13–61, http://www.jstor.org/stable/45205371.
4. Charles F. Swift, *History of Old Yarmouth, Massachusetts: Comprising the Present Towns of Yarmouth and Dennis* (Yarmouth Port, MA: Charles F. Swift, 1884; reprint: Salem, MA: Higginson Book, 1992), https://www.loc.gov/item/01015954/.

CHAPTER 3

Barnstable and Dennis—Traditions

1. Mercy Lord Taylor to Sylvanus Bourne, bill of sale written and signed on November 25, 1745, available in the Dennis Historical Society Digital Archives, catalog number 4800, viewed at Bill of Sale—4800 (catalogaccess.com).
2. Equal Justice Initiative, "The Transatlantic Slave Trade" (2022).
3. Richard Ligon, *True Exact History of the Island of Barbados* (London: Humphrey Mosely, 1657; Project Gutenberg, May 7, 2023), http://www.gutenberg.org/ebooks/70489.
4. Equal Justice Initiative, "The Transatlantic Slave Trade" (2022).
5. Helen Bourne J. Lee, *The Bourne Genealogy* (Quintin, 1972), 24.
6. Ibid.

CHAPTER 4

Eastham—Encounters and Economics

1. This document is in the public domain. Mayflower Compact, 1620, accessed at http://themayflowersociety.org/history/the-mayflower-compact/.
2. William Bradford, *Bradford's History of Plimoth Plantation* (Boston: Wright & Potter, 1898; Project Gutenberg, March 29, 2008), https://www.gutenberg.org/ebooks/24950.
3. Christopher Klein, "Why Did the Pilgrims Come to America?," History Channel, A&E Television Networks, November 13, 2020, https://www.history.com/news/why-pilgrims-came-to-america-mayflower.
4. Elizabeth Donnan, *Documents Illustrative of the History of the Slave Trade to America*, vol. 2 (Washington, DC: Carnegie Institution of Washington, 1931), https://archive.org/details/documentsillustr00donn_0.

CHAPTER 5

Brewster—Captains

1. J. Henry Sears, *Brewster Ship Masters* (Yarmouth Port, MA: C. W. Swift,

1906), https://books.google.com/books?id=yYMUAAAAYAAJ&pg=PP1#v=onepage&q&f=false.
2. Equal Justice Initiative, "The Transatlantic Slave Trade" (2022).
3. "Slavery & the Massachusetts Courts | Long Road to Justice," *Long Road to Justice: The African American Experience in the Massachusetts Courts*, accessed July 30, 2023, http://www.longroadtojustice.org/topics/slavery/.
4. Sears, *Brewster Ship Masters*.
5. Austin Bearse, *Reminiscences of Fugitive Slave Days in Boston* (Boston: Warren Richardson, 1880), https://books.google.com/books?id=eYtuULUUBHYC&pg=PP7#v=onepage&q&f=false.
6. Cobb quoted in Sears, *Brewster Ship Masters*, 15.
7. Edward L. Pierce, ed. *Memoir and Letters of Charles Sumner*. (Boston: Roberts Brothers, 1893), 179
8. Bearse, *Reminiscences of Fugitive Slave Days in Boston*.

CHAPTER 6
Falmouth and Mashpee—Fugitives

1. Catharine Sedgwick, manuscript draft in the collections of the Massachusetts Historical Society, http://www.masshist.org/database/viewer.php?item_id=547&image_step=1&pid=15&mode = dual#.
2. William Wells Brown, *Narrative of William Wells Brown, a Fugitive Slave* (Boston: Anti-Slavery Office, 1847), 84.
3. "The Underground Railroad," PBS, accessed July 28, 2023, https://www.pbs.org/wgbh/aia/part4/4p2944.html.
4. Brown, *Narrative of William Wells Brown, a Fugitive Slave*.

CHAPTER 7
Chatham and Harwich—Churches

1. Brown, *Narrative of William Wells Brown, a Fugitive Slave*, 97.
2. Cotton Mather, "The Negro Christianized: An Essay to Excite and Assist That Good Work, the Instruction of Negro-Servants in Christianity (1706)," Electronic Texts in American Studies, ed. Paul Royster, https://digitalcommons.unl.edu/etas/2.

3. Lucy Stone, letter to her mother, written from Oberlin College in 1849. Letter transcript found in the Library of Congress collections, viewed at https://crowd.loc.gov/campaigns/blackwells-extraordinary-family/lucy-stone-family-correspondence/.
4. Parker Pillsbury, letter to the *North Star* newspaper, December 5, 1850, https://www.wwhp.org/Resources/WomansRights/pillsbury_letter.html.
5. Parker Pillsbury, "The Harwich Mob," *The Liberator* (Boston), September 16, 1848, fairuse.org/the-liberator/1848/19/15/the-liberator/18-37.pdf.
6. Ibid.
7. Ibid.
8. Ibid.

CHAPTER 8
Orleans—Connections

1. John S. Marr and John T. Cathey, "New Hypothesis for the Cause of an Epidemic among Native Americans, New England, 1616–1619," *Emerging Infectious Diseases* 16, no. 2 (2010): 281–86, http://www.cdc.gov/EID/content/16/2/281.htm.
2. Simeon L. Deyo, ed., *History of Barnstable County, Massachusetts* (New York: Blake,1890), https://archive.org/details/historyofbarnsta00deyo.

CHAPTER 9
Wellfleet—Ships

1. Emily Donaldson, Lauren H. Laham, and Margie Coffin Brown, *Cultural Landscape Report and Outbuildings Historic Structures Report* (Boston: Olmsted Center for Landscape Preservation, National Park Service, 2010), nphistory.com/publications/caco/clr-atwood-higgins-pdf/.
2. "First Slaver Was Built in Marblehead," *Marblehead Messenger*, March 16, 1934, 2, https://marbleheadmuseum.org/ship-desire/.
3. Letter from Hugh Peter to John Winthrop, *Historical Magazine, and Notes and Queries Concerning the Antiquities, History and Biography of America* 7 (1863), https://archive.org/details/historicalmagaziv8morr/page/n3/mode/2up.

4. "First Slaver Was Built in Marblehead."
5. Donaldson, et al., *Cultural Landscape Report and Outbuildings Historic Structures Report*.
6. Trans-Atlantic Slave Trade Database, slavevoyages.org.

CHAPTER 10
Truro—Abolition

1. Earle, *Home Life in Colonial Days*, Internet Archive, https://archive.org/details/in.ernet.dli.2015.233561.
2. Shebnah Rich, *Truro—Cape Cod; or Land Marks and Sea Marks* (Boston: D. Lothrop, 1884), https://archive.org/stream/cu31924028839459/cu31924028839459_djvu.txt.
3. John Adams to Jeremy Belknap, March 21, 1795, https://founders.archives.gov/documents/Adams/99-02-02-1659.
4. James Otis, *The Rights of the British Colonies Asserted and Proved* (1764), available at www.teachingamericanhistory.org.
5. Links to documents available at https://www.mass.gov/guides/massachusetts-constitution-and-the-abolition-of-slavery.
6. Catharine Sedgwick, manuscript draft in the collections of the Massachusetts Historical Society, http://www.masshist.org/database/viewer.php?item_id=547&image_step=1&pid=15&mode = dual#.
7. Rich, *Truro—Cape Cod; or Land Marks and Sea Marks*.
8. Ibid.

CHAPTER 11
Provincetown to Bourne—Full Circle

1. Address of President Roosevelt on the Occasion of the Laying of the Cornerstone of the Pilgrim Memorial Monument, Provincetown, MA, August 20,1907, Project Gutenberg, May 12, 2022, https://www.guten berg.org/ebooks/68052.

Index of People and Places

Photo by Allison Graham

About the Author

Susanna Graham-Pye is an award-winning writer who has worked for over 30 years for most every publication on Cape Cod. She is a middle-school language arts and writing teacher. She has published one novel. During her career as a journalist, she received national, regional, and state recognition for her reporting.

Graham-Pye graduated from Smith College with a bachelor of arts and Goddard College with a master of fine arts in writing. She lives on Cape Cod with her family. She will continue her efforts to find and report on the lives of people who were enslaved and unremembered in the pages of Cape history.